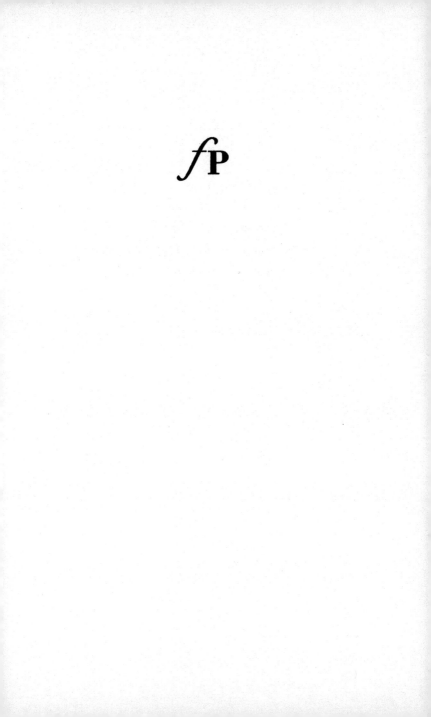

Also by Robert Rowland Smith

Breakfast with Socrates:
An Extraordinary (Philosophical) Journey
Through Your Ordinary Day

DRIVING
WITH
PLATO

The Meaning of Life's Milestones

ROBERT ROWLAND SMITH

FREE PRESS

New York   London   Toronto   Sydney

*f***P**

FREE PRESS
A Division of Simon & Schuster, Inc.
1230 Avenue of the Americas
New York, NY 10020

For information about special discounts for bulk purchases,
please contact Simon & Schuster Special Sales at 1-866-506-1949
or business@simonandschuster.com.

The Simon & Schuster Speakers Bureau can bring authors to your live event.
For more information or to book an event, contact the Simon & Schuster Speakers
Bureau at 1-866-248-3049 or visit our website at www.simonspeakers.com.

DESIGNED BY ERICH HOBBING

Manufactured in the United States of America

3   5   7   9   10   8   6   4   2

Library of Congress Cataloging-in-Publication Data

Smith, Robert Rowland.
Driving with Plato : the meaning of life's milestones / Robert Rowland
Smith.—1st Free Press hardcover ed.
p. cm.
1. Life. 2. Life change events. 3. Meaning (Philosophy) I. Title.
BD431.S59 2011
128—dc22
2010037548

ISBN 978-1-4391-8687-9
ISBN 978-1-4391-8689-3 (ebook)

To Zoë, Esther, and Eden,
as time goes by.

CONTENTS

CONTENTS

All the world's a stage,
And all the men and women merely players;
They have their exits and their entrances,
And one man in his time plays many parts,
His acts being seven ages. At first, the infant,
Mewling and puking in the nurse's arms.
Then the whining schoolboy, with his satchel
And shining morning face, creeping like snail
Unwillingly to school. And then the lover,
Sighing like furnace, with a woeful ballad
Made to his mistress' eyebrow. Then a soldier,
Full of strange oaths and bearded like the pard,
Jealous in honour, sudden and quick in quarrel,
Seeking the bubble reputation
Even in the cannon's mouth. And then the justice,
In fair round belly with good capon lined,
With eyes severe and beard of formal cut,
Full of wise saws and modern instances;
And so he plays his part. The sixth age shifts
Into the lean and slippered pantaloon
With spectacles on nose and pouch on side;
His youthful hose, well saved, a world too wide
For his shrunk shank, and his big manly voice,
Turning again toward childish treble, pipes

And whistles in his sound. Last scene of all,
That ends this strange eventful history,
Is second childishness and mere oblivion,
Sans teeth, sans eyes, sans taste, sans everything.

William Shakespeare,
As You Like It, Act II,
scene vii, lines 139–66

ACKNOWLEDGMENTS

Because *Driving with Plato* is the companion book to my *Breakfast with Socrates*, it benefits from the support of all those involved in that first publication. I thank them again. I'd also like to single out both my agent, Stephanie Ebdon at the Marsh Agency, and my editor, Daniel Crewe at Profile Books, along with their colleagues; I also thank Hilary Redmon at Free Press in New York. An author couldn't ask for better.

INTRODUCTION

Imagine getting into your car and finding that as soon as you switch on the engine, it turns into a time machine. But instead of pitching you backward and forward through the history of the planet, as did the famous contraption imagined by H. G. Wells, it zooms right in on your own life. It takes you back to bawling as a baby, noses through the gates of the school where you are taking a math lesson, and pulls over by a bus stop to study you as a teenager having your first kiss. It then accelerates toward your later years, to watch you floundering in a midlife crisis, say, or having a drink at your retirement party. And when death looms into view, the car doesn't just screech to a halt: it inches forward to have a look at what might lie beyond. That is the both ordinary and extraordinary journey taken by this book.

And you have company. You look to the passenger seat and notice none other than Plato, beard blowing in the wind. He's not just along for the ride, he's there to help you make sense of things. He observes you falling in love, for example, and explains how this very human experience connects you with the divine. Look behind into the backseat and, crammed in against the windows, you behold a whole team of writers, thinkers, painters, and other gurus, all eager to comment on what they see and offer insights about your life. Louis Althusser, the French Marxist, explains how those school gates might as well be the entrance to a prison. Leonardo da Vinci peeps at you losing your virginity and ponders how you'd measure up against the ideal of purity he painted in *The Virgin of the Rocks*. John Milton looks on as you go through an ugly divorce and consoles you that there's nothing to feel bad about— paradise can still be regained. You hear from Hegel on the matter of having children, Locke on the question of how those children learn to talk, and Tolstoy on how to control them so they don't talk too much. They are there, these luminaries from the history of ideas, like a raucous team of All Stars, to cajole, inform, caution, and entertain you as you pass each one of your milestones.

Many of these milestones are of course natural: being born, learning to walk, growing old, and dying. But just as many will be cultural, even if they've gained acceptance as near-inevitable rites of passage. These include starting school, passing your driving test, moving house, and getting married. Unlike the simplest animals, we don't merely eke out a biological fate, even if, like them, we're subject to laws of growth, hunger, decay, and reproduction. We create structures around us, be they material, like houses, or institutional, like schools and governments, which take on an endurance and an independence that belie their origins in the biological human that creates them. We're both natural and cultural creatures, and this book looks at both these interrelated aspects of our lives.

Decades of individualism have told us we're all unique, but we enjoy a largely common trajectory through the world. True, some people will become rich, many will live in penury, and plenty will strive throughout life merely to improve on the situation they were dealt at birth, but these differences in fortune rarely alter the basic path of life as it is lived. We're all born, we all connect with others, and we all die. Not all the milestones I discuss will be passed by everyone, and they may occur in a different order, but they should all be highly familiar if only from observing friends. The strange thing is that the familiarity isn't guaranteed to make them more intelligible: no matter how many weddings you attend, say, you might not have stepped back to think about their meaning, and even if you have, you might still find the ritual bizarre. One could even say that there can be something obscure about what's most common; the fact that we've all been to job interviews makes it likely that we take them for granted and don't ever get at the essence of what is going on. And so, in the company of various thinkers, this book examines what often remains unexamined in such events and phases. It helps you think a little deeper about the key moments and transitions in your life.

Some might argue that life flows more smoothly precisely by not analyzing it too much. But there are rewards in being able to reflect on these subjects, especially if the reflection is informed by the thinkers I've crammed into my car. (If they sound forbiddingly intellectual, I'm equally happy to cite *The Very Hungry Caterpillar, Thelma and Louise*, and the American sitcom *Curb Your Enthusiasm*.) Thinking through the philosophy of midlife crisis, for example, might help to forestall it. Appreciating what was involved in learning to walk and talk might make us more insightful parents. Examining the experience of being born will round out our sense of the miracle that it is. If life is a mystery, then let's take advantage of everything at our disposal to shed a little light. Besides, where asking about the meaning of life is too large a question to be helpful, breaking things down into life's milestones can give us a little bit of traction.

To drive with Plato is to take a fresh look at the moments that define the all too brief transit our car makes across the earth. There are some remarkable ideas to explore en route.

1

Being Born

Jean-Luc Godard, the doyen of avant-garde cinema, declared that every story needs a beginning, a middle, and an end—but not necessarily in that order. What about the story of your life?

If you're talking to a friend, you could start the story of your life with your first love or your last job, for example, and work forward or backward, making your story like any other story, subject to all sorts of cutting and pasting that undermines the notion of a simple beginning, middle, and end. You certainly don't have to begin with birth.

When it comes to your life as you live it, however, a different law applies: your life as lived is affixed to a chassis of biology, and the chassis's chassis is real time, which for you begins when you slither out of the womb. The story of your life and your life as lived denote two quite different things. On the one hand, there's your biological progress, and on the other hand, the edited version of that progress as narrated. In the spirit of Godard, Martin Amis once wrote a novel called *Time's Arrow*, which "begins" the story at the end and works back, but being a novel, of course it could. When it comes to living your life, that colored-in bar stretching from a starting to a finishing line, it can go only one way.

However you picture that starting point, a starting point is what the momentous event of birth emphatically is. Birth marks the beginning of life independent of umbilicus, placenta, and amniotic fluid. No one is actually born in their forties; if the prospect is so freakish, it's because life is only ever given to us from the beginning, its gift never secondhand or recycled, but always delivered brand new. To cite a classic storytelling device, a life that starts *in medias res* ("in the middle of things") is unimaginable: birth and beginning go hand in tiny hand. What's more, because it's the beginning of something (i.e., you), the creation of the uncreated, this beginning-energy is also a breaking-energy, a dislocation of the flat line along which a world-without-you would have otherwise continued. Your birth is the constructive interruption that alters the tableau of things, making it resize and reshuffle around your newborn self. More than the filling of a vacancy, this is the kneading into significant form of a formerly nothingish dot. In your own microcosmic way, you are a unique cosmic event, a little Big Bang.

That life begins at birth would appear to be one of the most solid facts we can start from, and yet since the advent of ultrasound technology and the opportunity it provides to peer inside the baby-bearing womb, our thoughts about when life begins have got rather muddled. While many continue to think of life beginning with birth, others say it starts with conception, and a few insist it begins somewhere between the two, in the slow-motion bloom of the fetus's consciousness—meaning that the front end of the colored bar has a gray area.

What makes that area gray isn't only the biology, as it happens, or even the ethics of abortion that dogs it: it's the philosophical question of whether, despite all this emphasis on starting points, yours is a beginning at all. Even though your expulsion from the mother's body jump-starts your career as a singleton, as an entity with edges de-soldered from anyone else, this effect of singularity stemmed from a cause—namely, the amorous clash of parental chromosomes. Unless yours was a virgin birth, you'll have had two biological parents, on whom your being born depended. Your "beginning" didn't come from nowhere—it was caused by something before you, meaning the singleness you achieve upon being born is something of an illusion; you are actually the result of a process that began long before your conception. The phrase *being born* suggests a launching into fresh individuality, but it could also be construed as the mere unfurling of the latest leaf on a very long stem whose base extends well back into history.

Similarly, the very notion of being "caused" by your parents might be subject to doubt. I'm thinking here of David Hume, luminary of the Scottish Enlightenment and arch-proponent of empiricism, the doctrine that puts direct observation above abstract theory. Hume was particularly exercised by the false or hasty conjoining of cause with effect, and his famous example was billiards: one ball strikes another with the predictable consequence of sending it off in a given direction. But once in a while something unexpected will happen, and the first ball will backfire, skid, or bounce. The lesson is that a single exception can invalidate the rule, so you have to consider each event on its merits; in this sense, theories are for the lazy, mere ready reckoners that help you slog along with a working, but imprecise, knowledge of the world. So what might be the empiricist attitude to birth? Every time a baby is born, you'd have to prove, rather than assume, that it was the fruit of two human loins.

If that sounds tedious or absurd, just remember that the virgin birth itself was an exception so compelling that it gave birth in turn to a world movement. Yet even the virgin birth was not without a cause, which, if you believe it, was the first cause of all: the Prime Mover of the world, otherwise known as God. Assuming God is the creator, his unique selling point would be that there's no cause that causes him, a marvel that medieval theologians called the *causa sui*. This makes being born—whether you're a creationist who traces it back through your parents to Adam and Eve, or just believe that all creation is God's own—a direct result of Him. As a deriving from God, and thus a deriving from something derived from nothing, this is the first of three senses in which birth can be seen as a miracle. The second sense would be as described by atheist parents who, dismissing divine intervention in their child's birth, nevertheless feel the wonder at this appearance of new life and the astonishment that from the simple sexual clasp of mother and father, a child, in all its complex, miniature perfection, is born. What about the third?

The third sense of the miracle of birth belongs to the baby itself. All of us were born—you wouldn't be reading and I wouldn't be writing this otherwise—but most will have forgotten the experience. Hardly surprising, given the evidence that earliest memories tend to come from the age of three. True, we can consult a huge amount of literature about childbirth, but it's mostly to do with the birth of other people. Even if your own birth was meticulously documented, such objective accounts hardly replace the subjective report that would be so valuable to have. This remains chronically elusive, and yet some people testify that they continue into much later life to dream about their own birth, a fact worth dwelling on in case these dreams give a clue as to the paradoxically forgettable experience of what is most seminal in our lives.

Birth dreams are not quite the same as memories, and leave a shadowy, *sentic* impression, more a feeling than an image; people speak of a sensation of pressure on the head, for example. Nor are they like such common dreams as being naked in public, which are painfully clear. These so-called birth dreams resemble occlusions of the soul, dark spots on the psyche that, like animals at night, just about stand out from the darkness that surrounds them. For these reasons, birth dreams correspond to what Plato called *anamnesis,* which, as the word suggests, is pretty much the opposite of amnesia. Except there's a crucial distinction, for Plato, between remembering and not forgetting: the latter harbors experiences in the mind without putting them in its grasp. This is anamnesis, and it's likely that birth dreams fall into this category: a not-forgetting, as opposed to a clear recollection, of what's beyond one's conscious reach. The memory of birth is gone, yet not completely lost.

Perhaps that's not so extraordinary. Why wouldn't you preserve, somewhere in your being, as in a fossil record, the trace of its founding event? To efface it would be weirder. It does imply, however, that whatever our age, we carry the whole of our biological past in the present, like a walking palimpsest of experience, or a cliff face in which each stratum, as you go down, speaks to an epoch older than the one above, and all are on show. If under the category of anamnesis Plato says you can intuit things you don't remember experiencing, or re-cognize what was never cognized the first time around, then being born provides the perfect material for it. It was an event that came upon you without you even knowing. It's in this that the miracle consists, the surprise from nowhere that inaugurates who you are.

To others, however, the miracle of birth is misery, the gift of life a curse, and with this we meet the empiricist's bête noire: existentialism. Whereas empiricism calls for vigilance over the detail of what is, existentialism draws the grandest conclusions about what is and is not; it treks beyond the annotating of activity in the foothills of experience to the high ground of generalization and the sweeping panoramas it affords. Take Jean-Paul Sartre, who would have said that being born is a poisoned chalice, because it offers you life but withholds the meaning to go with it, like winning a sports car and immediately losing the keys. For a start, being born was entirely out of your hands—the very origin of your life, and you didn't have a say in it! Birth happens to you, rather than your determining it, and that leaves you affronted by the arbitrariness of your own existence, which, in any case, could already be reduced to the chance encounter nine months earlier of Joe Sperm and Jane Egg. Not to mention the throw of the dice that made you appear in a random year, in a random location, and of a random gender, ethnicity, and class. Things scarcely improve as you grow up; anyone with eyes to see will observe how everything that happens happens as a result of equally arbitrary causes—an event as major as the First World War starts with a minor to-do about an Austrian duke, one thing leads to another, and hey presto, the dogs of war are let loose. There's obviously no God. Believing in one is just a comforting delusion, and so no overarching sense is to be made of anything. From birth you're consigned to beetling about on your patch of the forest floor, moving twigs from *A* to *B*.

For all that, Sartre manages to pull something from the fire, realizing that precisely because there's no transcendent meaning, there's no bar on creating one for yourself. If being born is an inauspicious fall into a mire of meaninglessness, you can rationalize it as a necessary preparation for a great life that might ensue—a greatness that can't, however, be left to chance. In response to the classification in *Twelfth Night* that "some are born great, some achieve greatness, and some have greatness thrust upon them," Sartre would have rejected categories 1 and 3: you've got to make your own luck, and you do so, above all, by redeeming the accident of your birth and taking it upon yourself to act. Part of this philosopher's appeal to the class of '68 who rioted in the streets of Paris (the very streets that Jean-Luc Godard had just been filming) was his antiphilosophical emphasis on action as a means of giving life a purpose—an emphasis he'd borrowed from Karl Marx, who claimed, "So far philosophers have only interpreted the world—the point is to change it!"

But you don't have to be so brazen. Being born has a number of natural consolations. Not only do you get to live, but because, before birth, you weren't living at all, you also might have a useful inkling of what's to come on the other side. The time before birth could be a rehearsal for the time after life (or death, not to beat about the bush), which should relax any fear of dying that grips you. And even if Sartre is right, and being born means being cast into a landscape of hopeless contingency, there's another way of looking at it. While he said you're morally required to convert the position you find yourself in at birth, of being merely *en-soi* ("in yourself") into being *pour-soi,* or "for yourself," thus making the passive active, his opposite number in Germany, Martin Heidegger, saw pretty much the reverse.

First of all, you can't be without being somewhere, and when you're born, you take up space on the planet and in a particular geography. All being, therefore, is being-there, connected to the earth. Far from getting cut adrift in a Sartrean wasteland, being born means finding a place, and belonging.

Second, if your being has to exist in a place, it also has to exist in time; being born means entering time's river, so to speak. Rather than, as in Sartre, having to grope for a sense of direction, you are from the moment you're born, directed in time, taken forward in an element or medium that activates your being—after all, if you didn't exist in time, you'd be as frozen as a statue. Taken together, that means birth is the gift of time and space, the two main facets of being. Before birth, you have neither, but your coming into the world means being presented with everything that is.

2

Learning to Walk and Talk

What goes on four legs in the morning, two at midday, and three in the evening? If you don't know, I'll kill you. If you do, I'll kill myself.

Such was the riddle of the Sphinx, the mythical monster who perched crazily at the city limits of Thebes in ancient Greece, tormenting passersby with its exorbitant wager. Before the riddle was solved, many fell foul of the half-human, half-lion freak. When it was, its decoder was none other than Oedipus. His answer, of course, was *man*, the creature that in its infancy crawls, walks upright in the middle of its life, and in its third age resorts to a walking stick. On hearing Oedipus's suave reply, the sphinx, true to its word, dashed itself to the ground in an act of self-murder.

Beneath the horrors, the sphinx's cruel game alludes to the profound connection between man and walking. In the riddle, *man*—for which let's also read *woman*—gets defined by his ability to move about on his pins. Where the sphinx was four-legged (was her motive jealousy?), man is a biped, and as we'll see in a moment, that comes with advantages both theological and evolutionary. Whatever else he may be, man is a walker, a perambulator, a pedestrian. So when, as a baby, you haul yourself off your haunches to wobble on your soft pods, one hand on the sofa, you're doing more than reaching for the biscuit on Mom's plate—you are joining the species proper.

Not that this is the would-be toddler's conscious intent. Like the birth that preceded it roughly twelve months earlier, when, with a seismic convulsion, the mother's body was activated like an alarm clock to heave the suckling out onto the earth, in almost complete disregard for her will, nothing can brook this urge to stand and move. More powerful than the baby itself, a force passes through it, calling it with all the imperiousness of Jesus commanding Lazarus, to stand up and walk. True, the baby in the moment might use its muscles deliberately and will control its movements as best it can, but this urge on the ground comes from one higher up: the biological imperative that makes our bodies grow, develop, and assume a certain shape. No matter how feeble the fledgling attempts, how often the little one falls back on its bottom, walking will happen soon enough. Unless there's a defect of some kind, it's perfectly unstoppable.

Consider: What if it were a force you could resist, and you never learned to walk at all? Apart from having to eat dust and forfeiting the entire vertical plane for moving about in—that is, losing a whole dimension—you'd find yourself on the lowest echelon of a stairway to heaven. It's sometimes forgotten that the snake in the Garden of Eden, the devil incarnate, was originally able to walk upright. Being damned to crawl on its belly was the snake's punishment for tempting Eve, which turned it into the literal embodiment of a lowly form of life, the subtle serpent become a humble worm. And if that's life on the bottom rung of the stairway, the realm of beings that crawl, then having the ability to walk—the next rung up—must be a privilege. Walking doesn't only define man, it speaks to a superiority on his part that's to do with more than physical elevation. The altitude achieved in standing up speaks to his nearness to God and corresponding distance from the animals, such that the height of the head of the standing human marks the symbolic midpoint between heaven and earth. When that person then starts to move by walking through its extra dimension, a gift of liberty is redeemed, a liberty not just geographical but scientific: walking offers the opportunity for surveying new worlds.

Yet both crawling and walking find themselves outdone in turn by what's possible from the top rung of the stairway: flying. Yes, walking testifies to freedom, but of a circumscribed variety that falls somewhat short of the airy transport favored by the angels who look down on man and devil both. Although walking allows us to traverse the earth, it binds us to it, hence the name of the first man in that fateful garden. *Adam* means "red earth," implying that man was made of clay to curb any hubris of the kind that gave Satan ideas above his station; the word *human* also refers back to the soil. Man's feet were to remain on earth, as if that one extra dimension was privilege enough. Above him, and keeping him in his place, were the *putti* that floated about in celestial joy, unburdened from the supposed liberation of human walking that, compared with their own boundarylessness, must have seemed about as free as the plod of a chain gang.

To one angel, however, flying itself constitutes a burden, and walking is to be envied. I'm thinking of the German film of 1987 *Wings of Desire*, in which an angel becomes enamored with an earthling and longs to fall back to earth in order to be with her. But it's not just love he's after. Being bound to the earth brings rewards unavailable in heaven, to do with human emotion in all its imperfect complexity. For example, if you can fly like an angel, falling over holds no fear, whereas because we humans have had to learn to walk, and fallen over many times in the attempt, we have a more nuanced, more real sense of its value. To us, walking is a conquest over stumbling and slipping, over gravity itself and those countervailing forces we're always having to subdue. While the angel can hover above it in serene immunity, walking puts us into tension with the earth, and that brings a certain human satisfaction.

What's more, where angels are either invisible or, on being glimpsed, liable to vanish into thin air, walking leaves a trace. The baby's first steps, though in one sense generic, signal the beginning of a journey that moves in a particular direction that can't be undone and remains a unique document of its progress. Going where angels never tread makes a path in time, and when you learn to walk you are marking your place on the earth, scratching your autobiography into the ground. Zora Neale Hurston, the great African American chronicler, gave her 1942 autobiography the title *Dust Tracks on a Road*, and this idea of walking your life has been brought out more recently by the British landscape artist Richard Long, who has spent his career crossing the mountains and valleys of the earth on foot. While he builds stone circles and records his journeys in both photographs and semipoetic journal entries, thus turning them into art objects, the walks themselves also lay claim to being pieces of art. Or rather, they are pieces of nature that show how the act of walking merges with the art of being human and plots our relationship to the dust from which we've come and to which we'll return.

All of which reinforces the idea that walking makes

the human human. Even the theory of evolution, which reminds us that we are monkeys and, in doing so, asks us to abandon the illusion of man's special relationship with God, compensates by showing how far we've surpassed those simian cousins. *Homo erectus* marks a triumph. When Darwin writes "I can see no reason why it should not have been advantageous to the progenitors of man to have become more and more erect and bipedal," there's a clear presumption that walking makes sense in competitive terms, and a suggestion that the becoming bipedal of the hominid, the movement that will ultimately extend from *Homo erectus* to *Homo sapiens*, marks a literal step toward intelligence. One can't help thinking the brain becomes more rangy and capable when set atop a neck, looking out like a periscope, rather than when mounted behind a snout truffling about on the ground. The one-year-old who can survey its new dominion has an undeniable advantage over the six-month-old baby who lies on its back flailing like a fly. It can look down as well as up, and that supplies it with an extra axis for appraising the world.

In Darwin, walking appears cognate with becoming human, and in this light the baby's advance from four to two legs reprises evolution itself, a kind of fractal echo. Yet one of Darwin's canniest revisionists, Elaine Morgan, says there's archaeological evidence proving the creature that went on to become *Homo erectus* was walking a long time before it became *man*, the mammal that could manipulate tools. The evolutionary chain included a bipedal animal that wasn't yet man, implying that the link between walking and humanness might not be so tight, and that insofar as we are bipeds, we humans fall into the same category as creatures as quirky as the ostrich.

Then, in a quite different rewriting of evolutionary theory, you have the teachings of F. Matthias Alexander, founder of the Alexander technique, which among other things alleviates backache through better posture. Making his observations in the late nineteenth century, Alexander noticed that our notions of "walking properly" were based on the idea that man is an upright animal, a creature with an almost militarily stiff bearing—and that this idea was culturally determined. If our parents and schoolteachers tell us to stand up straight, their words function partly to reassert the rectitude of the human being, but what Alexander suspected was that we hadn't evolved quite as far as we might have hoped. It is more natural, he suggested, for the knees to remain slightly bent, not locked, and for the spine to be flat, as opposed to curving out at the coccyx like a sergeant major's; the same applies to walking. The unavoidable implication is that, far from thrusting out the chest and holding up the chin, it's better and more appropriate for us to walk a little like the apes we so blithely assume we've overtaken. As it happens, Alexander used the technique to cure his own malady; an actor who lost his voice, he was informed that he'd never speak again, but by flattening his spine and letting his neck incline somewhat, he enabled his larynx to open again and fill with words.

No matter how natural and inevitable, however, the baby's first steps can't help being somewhat theatrical. Learning to walk rarely happens when one is alone; usually it takes place in a domestic theater of relatives urging you on and applauding each faltering, incremental advance, perhaps wielding a camera to capture you for posterity. It's a rite of passage that, unlike losing your virginity (exhibitionists excepted), will almost certainly happen in view of others. And once you've mastered it, walking remains a going forth; unless you're the anxious type, given to pacing the floorboards, you won't walk about very much indoors. It nearly always means being out in the world and passing under other eyes.

In this sense, learning to walk forms part of a baby's social, not just its motor, development. There's an obvious way in which making physical contact with another person requires crossing the room; it's usually the feet that enable the touching of hands. But true socialization, it is thought, comes with the acquisition of language, and among language's myriad benefits, one is that you can touch others without having to touch them and move them without having to move them. Talking spares us a lot of walking. That it acts at a distance both characterizes language and lends it power. It's something the baby knows long before it has molded any words in its mouth, for its cry was designed to project vital needs over the longest possible range, as if the volume of its cry lay in direct proportion to its inability to walk. As the cry gradually morphs into language, the volume of oral emissions goes down and their precision goes up.

That transition from crying to talking doesn't happen overnight; it involves a period of babble, and if there's a theological depth to walking, then the biblical roots of speaking run deeper still. Getting up and walking might have afforded man a certain height and raised him closer to God, but such terrestrial stretching was spectacularly exceeded by the Tower of Babel. Constructed with the explicit aim of reaching into the heavens and broadcasting the skill of those who had built it, it stood as a monument to mankind's self-love. Until, that is, God in righteous indignation demolished it, scattering its inhabitants to the four corners of the earth. With their dispersal came the curse of speaking different tongues and ever after hearing their former compatriots' words as mere "babble." Not that *Babel* and *babble* are strictly related: no connection with Babel has been reliably established. However, both Babel and babble, in this woeful allegory, refer to a state of being cut off from others. There are times when the babble of a baby can seem demented, not so much a form of nascent expression as impenetrable solipsism; babble is subjective expression that defeats objective understanding, leaving the infant stranded in a halfway house between private articulation and public incomprehension.

To a school of postwar literary theorists, however, babble marks a particularly precious phase, something to cherish rather than develop away from. Because social norms have yet to correct it, baby babble represents the point at which language is most redolent with desire, with unfettered longing. In this it's almost like poetry or dreamspeak, that interior monologue that falls under the radar of our conscious selves. To witness a baby burbling might be to tune into its unconscious, inner life, into a narrative of unimpeded desire. In fact the toddler's pleasure in its ululations, and the disregard for conformity, hint at other kinds of subversion. It will sound far-fetched, but in the eyes of some theorists, babble has political potential because it's untamed language that literally speaks to its speaker's disregard for what is and is not acceptable. It's a self-indulgent pleasure that defies the efforts of elders—for which read "the state"—to constrain it. Before long, however, we do conform: our language becomes "normal" and we articulate the world in the way that those around us do. There's a gain in being understood and accepted, but a loss in leaving behind those aspects of the world that now lie beyond the reach of the newly acquired linguistic faculty.

Babble might even reveal something of the origin of language itself, something that James Joyce tried to reproduce in *Finnegans Wake*. Take the opening of the third paragraph:

> The fall (bababadalgharaghtakamminarronnkonnbron ntonnerronntuonnthunntrovarrhounawnskawntoohoo hoordenenthurnuk!) of a once wallstrait oldparr is related early in bed and later on life down through all christian minstrelsy.

It might, like a baby's babble, sound like nonsense, but it's packed with allusion, not least to the idea of the fall of man, and in particular of that fall from the Tower of Babel into the melee of languages we're then consigned to disentangle. (Joyce said people should spend their entire lives studying his work.) Like Joyce's text, a baby's babble can actually be understood as a strangely integrated language, whole and consistent, a discourse that prevailed before the dispersal of tongues, the multiplication of new languages, and the burden of having to translate between them. Alternatively, but also like Joyce, babble might represent that very confusion that arose after Babel and the hell of misunderstanding. If the latter, we can hear the baby's burbling as a lament for the fact of having to enter the world of compromise and negotiation, of social relations and grammatical order. The baby "falls" into language and out of the Edenic state of simply being.

But a fall into language implies that the baby has no language before the fall, that its brain is empty, which raises an important philosophical question. For if a baby arrived on earth with nothing in its head, how would it know about eternal values like truth and goodness? How would it acquire reason? Yes, it could find out about these over time, but if they had to be learned from other humans, from adults, this would imply that those eternal truths were not so eternal. They would be the mere product of experience accumulated by others who came before, pragmatic constructs rather than transcendent principles—a possibility abhorrent to classical philosophy. Instead, learning to talk surely must be a process that gradually excavates and activates the language embedded in the baby's mind from birth; its parents might nudge it along, but the language was already there, waiting to be teased out. To use a technical simile, the newborn's brain is like a computer preinstalled with software.

Not surprisingly, this classical view had its critics, and chief among them was John Locke, the eighteenth-century philosopher and political radical. Like David Hume, whom we caught playing billiards in the previous chapter, Locke was a keen empiricist. He compared the baby's mind to a *tabula rasa*, or blank sheet of paper. When you learned to talk you were taking in simple ideas from the world about you, then combining them in your mind to make those ideas more complex, and finally expressing them in words. Rather than being imposed on you, your language was a reflection of your experience as you lived it. In fact, experience would provide the source and the limits of all your knowledge, such that your language would always be autobiographical, a palimpsest of everything you had witnessed. Locke's riposte also helps to explain babble, for by his account all language becomes fundamentally subjective, a processing of life as lived from one's own unique perspective. If the babble gives way to recognizable language, that language represents the reconciliation of all the babbles spoken by everyone. Today we say babies' brains are "sponges" that soak up everything around them; the metaphor is one upon which Locke would have smiled.

Halfway between the classicists and Locke comes the argument made most famously by Noam Chomsky, the American-based professor of linguistics. Although unpersuaded by the idea of divine knowledge, he does hold that the baby's brain comes with a limited set of verbal tricks, which it proceeds to enrich according to the context. It might come equipped with stock phrases, like "I am here" or "I like it," and these can be adapted to make longer phrases, like "I am here in my house" or "I like this food." And so the baby becomes capable of expressing more and more complex realities ("I like the food in my house").

But if expressing things in words suggests that language is principally an instrument for articulating a thought, we should think again. True, that is how language has been very largely conceived throughout the history of ideas. And yet you could also turn that logic upside down. When a baby looks at a banana and names it, it might be that it's the naming that causes the understanding rather than the other way around. Think of how learning the name of a flower, for example, and then mouthing the word helps us see it anew. To speak is not just to express but to impress a meaning on things, and in this, interestingly, it resembles walking, which is itself a way of stamping a path on the earth and so giving it an intelligible pattern. Both walking and talking are ways of measuring the world, of breaking it down into units, be they yards or words. And with measuring comes understanding.

3

Starting School

"My Old School," the Steely Dan hit of the 1970s, features the following lines, "California tumbles into the sea/That'll be the day I go/Back to Annandale." How come school can be such a drag?

Partly because it's an entirely artificial construct. Consider the egregious difference between this third chapter and the two before: whereas being born and learning to walk and talk are natural, practically irresistible processes, starting school is the first purely cultural milestone we must pass. There's nothing organic about it at all: one doesn't start school in the same way that one begins to grow armpit hair or wisdom teeth, and classmates are not biological extensions of the self. If starting school is a milestone, therefore, it's one that could have been bypassed, and the fact that it's almost universal shouldn't hoodwink us into thinking otherwise. Starting school starts you down a particular track, like turning right at a crossroads instead of driving straight ahead.

For *had* you driven straight on, the orthodoxy says, you might have got lost in the bogs and woods of wild childhood, doomed to remain not just uneducated, but untamed. At least, this is the negative myth that schooling silently endorses: the unschooled child is the savage child, and to deter that uncouth possibility, school imposes itself on your early life. It thereby makes a radical intervention, perhaps the first you properly experience, an abrupt correction by external forces of your default momentum. This might explain why it can create such an impression on you, sometimes traumatically so (a point I'll come back to), for the idea is that school helps you overcome your childhood rawness, helps you put your animal instincts in abeyance while the higher human capabilities are brought out. The word *education* means "leading out," exactly as if you had to be drawn away from the perils of that swamp.

To put it in the terms of the French Marxist critic Louis Althusser, starting school means being rescued and rehabilitated by the state, surrendering to its formidable dominion, and becoming a tool of ideology. Up to a point, school is everything it seems to be—what Althusser calls the learning of a number of techniques. But beyond that, things get more sinister:

> Besides these techniques and knowledges, and in learning them, children at school also learn the "rules" of good behaviour, i.e. the attitude that should be observed by every agent in the division of labour, according to the job he is "destined" for: rules of morality, civic and professional conscience, which actually means rules of respect for the socio-technical division of labour and ultimately the rules of the order established by class domination. They also learn to "speak proper French," to "handle" the workers correctly, i.e. actually (for the future capitalists and their servants) to "order them about" properly, i.e. (ideally) to "speak to them" in the right way, etc.

And you thought schooldays were the best days of your life! When you start school, you are not, as liberals and educational theorists would have you believe, embarking on a journey of academic attainment and personal development so much as being indoctrinated into a set of cultural practices whose aim is to uphold and prolong a capitalist system. More than just an intervention in your life, starting school adds up to what Althusser elsewhere calls an *interpellation*, a moment of being defined by political forces beyond your reach. In tandem with that political goal goes an economic one, whereby school seeks to channel students into the right slots for future labor. Which brings new meaning to the phrase *behaving in class*, that is, making sure you act in a way that corresponds with the class structure of society, not just the classroom. What's worse, those behaviors demanded by school are designed to blunt any criticism of them you might produce.

In this view, school becomes an Althusserian "ideological state apparatus," an institution designed to regulate behavior, reduce dissidence, and generate a labor force that settles into a class hierarchy with an ease that makes it appear natural. The techniques you learn aim more at reducing potential deviation from the norm—it being easier for the state to control subjects who are all more or less the same. Perhaps, writing in mid-twentieth-century France, Althusser had particular cause: it's said that at its zenith, state education in France meant that wherever you found yourself in L'Hexagon, all thirteen-year-olds, say, would be taking the same lesson at the same time, with the same textbooks and the same exercises. You could set your watch according to when they were all reading Racine.

You might bridle at the cool militancy of Althusser's

analysis or dismiss it for being as ideological as the ideology he critiques, but it does help account for the terrible jolt we perhaps felt on our first day at school. For even if you had been attending a preschool of some kind, the locus of your daily life would most probably have been the home, with all the comfort that suggests. Your identity in these infant years would have been that of a little person to be looked after, played with, cuddled, dandled on the loving lap of your elders. Your world was one of upholstered spaces and indulgences, a world of play overseen by a benign grownup, in the company of your own toys. And whenever anything went wrong, you had personal attention on tap, in the shape of that parent or caregiver, to make things all right. Then overnight your life is transformed, the familiar family exchanged for the strange squadrons of school, the soft furnishings for hard tables and desks, the day's seamless, spacey rhythm for the metronome of the school timetable. The new system is a shock to the system.

Although home had routines of its own, like bath time and bedtime, and prohibitions like not eating on the sofa, at school you come up against, in the form of school rules, a whole legislature that to a newbie appears as magisterial and barely decipherable as the inscriptions on a pyramid. It's precisely in these school rules that Althusser's abstract point becomes experientially real, for what makes school such a steep step up into the mature world is being confronted with exactly such a set of prescriptions and proscriptions you're obliged to observe. Having been given what felt like a free rein at home—even if you were subtly bound by a domestic set of codes—you are confronted anew at school with a direct sense of your being, and needing to be, controlled.

With this comes the more discombobulating than soothing sense that the rules themselves, so stentorian at one level, are, if not exactly silly, then certainly rather arbitrary. Not only did school not have to happen, but it didn't have to develop in the way it did, with its own peculiar customs. One of the most precious things about your first day at school is that you can still notice this. There's a proverb in management theory regarding organizations, "Culture is that which you stop noticing after three months," and it applies equally to starting school. Of course, at the age of four or five you don't have the wherewithal to surface your sense of that arbitrariness or articulate it as a challenge to the prevailing norm, though it's a precious resource, a way of looking at the world and seeing that it could have been entirely otherwise. And so school cultures go largely unchallenged. The arbitrary becomes the norm, and after those first few months you will not only have embraced it, but will believe it's the obvious way of spending your day.

Least challengeable of all must be the figure of the tyrannical schoolteacher, whose authority tolerates little resistance: for schoolteacher, read "sovereign." Think of Tolstoy's semiautobiographical account of the demon teacher in his story *Childhood*: "He ordered me to go down upon my knees, declared that it was all obstinacy and 'puppet-comedy playing' (a favourite expression of his) on my part, threatened me with the ruler, and commanded me to say that I was sorry."

The poor boy has clearly broken a rule, but as to which rule it is, he's unsure. The arbitrariness of the rule merges with the authority of the teacher, and together they generate a level of intimidation the boy could never withstand. His only recourse is to store the episode in his memory for later relating in a novel, as if in revenge. Until then, there's little the boy can do to protest. Indeed protest itself would be interpreted as further evidence of disobedience. What matters, in any case, is not the rationality or otherwise of the rules, still less their content; it's simply, for the schoolmaster, the imposing of them, and for the pupil, obedience. Thus a mini-empire is born, a foreign territory delimited by the iconic school gates that mark the transition to a different jurisdiction. It's something one feels even as a parent collecting one's little treasure: you might well be the parent, and therefore the ultimate authority over the child, but when you're on the school grounds that authority wobbles and, as if you'd passed through the Iron Curtain, you need to be on the lookout for rules you might be flouting.

But perhaps most disorienting of all in the experience of starting school is neither the shock of the new nor the anxiety stirred up by the arbitrariness of the regime you must now fall in with; it's the change in how you are perceived. In a sense your identity splits, and, to use the phrase of Althusser's younger philosophical compatriot, Paul Ricoeur, you become *yourself as another.* Up until your first day, you experience yourself as a reasonably undivided creature, which is to say that you don't really experience yourself at all. You simply are. You look at picture books, you go shopping with your mom, you play games on the carpet, you eat your snack. In Ricoeur's terms, you have at this stage an *idem* identity, but not yet any *ipse.* (In Latin, *idem* means "same" and *ipse* means "self," though Ricoeur is using them in an expanded sense.) That is, at home you fall in with the rhythm of things, with very little self-consciousness and little call for you to take any particular action or to reflect upon it afterward. Idem is all you are.

Once you start school, however, you are positioned as someone who needs to act responsibly, and this precipitates your ipse identity, or *ipseity*. No matter your years, from the moment you start school you are thought of as someone capable of exercising choice and whose actions stem from conscious intention. If you kick a ball through the window, you haven't merely made a mistake—which would be idem behavior—you've exercised a degree of will, an ipse action that renders you accountable. It's precisely the assumption that Tolstoy's schoolmaster is working on: whereas the little boy lingers in the world of the idem—he's simply bobbing along on the current, with limited sense of himself as a social agent—the teacher has him tagged as an ipse, which means the boy's every act can be weighed. The effect for the child is to see himself through the eyes of others, and especially those others who expect a certain level of conscientiousness. While this turnabout in perception counts among the more unsettling experiences that starting school brings, saddling you with a whole new dimension to manage, it delivers, on the other hand, some social and personal benefit. For if you think of school as a bridge between home and society, then perhaps being clad with some ipseity, represented in the school uniform, is no bad thing. Reflecting back to you the possibility that you have some ipseity is a way of preparing you to become a good citizen.

This change in how you are perceived that accompanies starting school goes hand in hand with how you are organized. Owing to the simple fact that schools contain more children than teachers, it makes sense, logistically, to treat those children in groups rather than singly. No longer the special one you were at home, you become one among many, a face in the crowd; you may well have a unique personality that needs attending to, or a set of special requirements, but when it comes to starting school you must, before anything else, be organized. And so you're redefined as a unit as well as a person, and rather as they would be in an army, your movements perfectly coordinated.

You are counted in and out; such is the emphasis on being present and the rigor with which absence gets catalogued. No doubt this conflicts with ipseity: on the one hand, you're asked to take responsibility; on the other, you're just a number. But when it comes down to it, being a number probably has more weight. Think of the sheer efficiency required to process several hundred kids through their school lunches or to get them to be in the right place at the right time for the next lesson, and you begin to realize that, as the driving force of the institution, *education* might come second to *operation*.

Apart from further eroding your sense of individuality, two consequences follow. The first is a loss of privacy. Whereas home had its retreats like the bedroom or that nook under the stairs—and there were times during the day when your caregiver was only too happy to stop watching over you—being constantly monitored means losing the option of hiding away. Even going to the toilet requires permission. It's as if the lives of children are common property, which perhaps helps explain why we associate privacy with adulthood. Be it in class, in the playground, or changing for PE, you do everything under the eyes of others.

But if being grouped, managed, and observed has behind it this operational necessity, a second, deeper factor applies that goes back to the very theory of knowledge, which itself goes back to medieval scholasticism, which goes back to Aristotle. There's a clue in the word *class*, though not in the Althusserian sense. The fact that being put in a class is the first thing that happens to you at school gives a clue as to how important classing is: the classes reflect how knowledge, and not just the students, must be organized. *That* knowledge must be organized, rather than swallowed whole, is the key point. It's the breaking down and classing of data into formal units that marks the first step toward the knowing of them. Everything from friendship to freedom Aristotle disaggregated into categories, because once you have categories you have things to compare and collate, and reasoning can commence. Say, for example, that somebody asked you to write an essay about school. You begin by dividing the topic into primary and secondary education, and you're off. With classification, knowledge begins, and once knowledge is put into classes—law, history, politics, math, and so on—the students follow into those divisions.

Long after Aristotle's era in the fourth century BC, his method was revived and redoubled, culminating in the great flowering of the school in the Middle Ages. Education starts to assume a form that anticipates the modern world, with knowledge broken down into "subjects" and the figure of the "master" whose expertise will guide you through them. Even today, when you start school you are essentially following this medieval conception of knowledge as separate subjects rather than a single holistic entity. Now we have the three Rs of reading, writing, and 'rithmetic, a clear echo of the medieval breakdown into the *trivium* (grammar, logic, and rhetoric) and the *quadrivium* (arithmetic, geometry, astronomy, and music). If on Day One at school you enter a class or grade, it might be less for Althusserian reasons—as an incipient and insidious form of the division of labor—than because the very architecture of knowledge demands it.

Once you comprehend this huge power of classification, you're better placed to understand the phenomenon of the school timetable: a representation in time of the tabulation of knowledge in general. Knowing where to be at what time for a lesson means, besides being operationally directed, that you are tracking across the very grid of knowledge. Your faint but constant sense at school of being routed around a circuit, like a train on a rail network, is actually an experience of being moved across a map of reason that was established hundreds of years ago. That the curriculum gets so tirelessly fiddled with by politicians makes no odds: the underlying concept remains that of the division of knowledge.

Against all these scenarios of rules and regulations, of rigorous divisions and academic hygiene, thankfully a strong countercurrent flows. Though the experience of starting school today preserves many of those formalities, a new doctrine of *personalization* has gained currency. Instead of fitting into the school, as in the old model, the school now has to fit around the child. In practice, no timetable can flex sufficiently to meet the individual needs of every student, and it wouldn't be a timetable if it did. So personalization has more to do with helping the child navigate the system in a way that reduces its scariness. After centuries of schooling, we're only just appreciating that fear isn't so conducive to learning, even if it helps with discipline; there's a sea change going on whereby the school becomes less a house of correction and more a home for personal development, just as those liberals had wished.

When it comes to the momentous event of starting

school, this modern doctrine results in, among other things, lowering the gradient of that child's entrance into it. Go to pretty much any Western city and you'll discover a host of preschool institutions and initiatives that help prepare the child for starting in Reception, as it's widely and revealingly known. As that other common word in Europe, *Kindergarten*, suggests, the beginning of school should emulate a garden for children, who implicitly will be allowed to play outside a little longer, as if they were still at home, before being called in for their lessons proper. Not that this relative leniency comes from educational theorists turning soft: behind it lies an evidence-based theory that the more emotionally settled the child, the more he or she is likely to learn, and therefore to attain. Because this also reflects well on the school and indeed on the state, it could be, in Althusserian terms, just a more subtle form of ideological manipulation. Even so, it improves the experience for the new kid at school, who can now look forward to joining a system that, alongside its educational goals, seeks as much to make him or her happy.

This countercurrent enjoys a tradition of its own, going back not quite as far as Aristotle, but at least to the eighteenth century of Jean-Jacques Rousseau. Writing at the high-water mark of Romanticism, which extolled self-expression, and during the French Revolution, which extolled liberty percolating up through the grassroots of society, Rousseau was pitched perfectly to articulate a set of ideals about how to secure the potential of human beings. He too was alive to the arbitrary authoritarianism of schools, which at its crudest rested on the fact that teachers were physically bigger than children. Those ideals would involve the easing of the bonds of society itself, which would always tend to corrupt our natural, even divine capacity to live as ennobled and enlightened creatures. Not surprisingly, they also extended to a theory of education, a theory we owe a great deal for our modern sense of the child as a creative entity, whose self-expression the school is there to facilitate rather than suppress in the name of accumulating exam passes. Their most obvious manifestation today might be the replacement of learning Latin by rote with, say, group discussion about ethics. They also inform the more liberal establishments associated with the names Maria Montessori and Rudolf Steiner.

But from these belated elaborations of Rousseau's thinking we shouldn't necessarily infer that school has to exist at all—and so we come back full circle to the idea of letting the child walk straight on into the woods. If nature holds the keys to the good life, and school is unnatural, it follows that the child ought to be allowed to pursue its own growth, like a wildflower whose seeds should be scattered far from the manicured lawn of educational institutions. In all cases—be it Althusser, Rousseau, or modern experts in education—the strange thing is that no matter how personal and immediate starting school might subjectively feel, what you're experiencing is the manifestation of a set of political and philosophical choices; hence that feeling of being small among big things, a Lilliputian. What you enter when you walk into school for the first time is not just an unfamiliar building and an unknown culture, but a battleground for the educational disagreements of your elders.

4

Learning to Ride a Bike

The Nobel laureate J. M. Coetzee is well-known for books that disregard the barrier between fact and fiction. So much so that it's hotly debated whether his novels *Boyhood, Youth,* and *Summertime* count as novels at all, so autobiographical is their material. Even in the less contested works, the ambiguity persists. *Slow Man,* for example, relates the story of a man recovering from a bicycle accident; in real life, Coetzee is said to be a keen cyclist, given to extended rides around his adopted city of Adelaide, Australia.

Like all accidents, the one that befalls Paul Rayment, Coetzee's alter ego, was not foreseen. Turning out of a side road onto a thoroughfare, he is sent flying from his bike by a sports car driven by a much younger and very different man. The random collision between the two men leads, novelistically, to further, less kinetic connections, but that doesn't change the fact that it leaves the protagonist needing a leg amputation. Hence the "slow man" of the title, which throws the relative speed of cycling into relief. Rayment wasn't a mere pedestrian, but a cyclist, and so becoming an amputee has meant dropping not only one leg, but two levels of speed. Barring motorized transport, cycling, along with skiing, is about as fast across earth as you can go.

It's worth noting an oddity that Coetzee's novel highlights, namely, that there's something ever so slightly unright about an older man—as opposed to a boy—on a bike. As he goes under the surgeon's saw, Rayment subliminally transmits the message that for him, an aging gentleman, to be cycling at all was foolish, even a little vain. He should have chosen transport more fitting for his age, with cycling reserved for the earlier, not the later, memoirs. Implicitly cycling should be for children; you could even say it's *about* children, about the abandon that childhood abounds in. What makes cycling so definitively an activity of childhood? Partly that, unlike Rayment's nemesis in the sports car, young children aren't allowed to drive, nor do they go very much by themselves on public transport. Other than walking and running, children don't have the options for getting about enjoyed by their seniors, so for want of choice they turn to the bicycle, and learn to love it.

Except that kids don't much need to get about. When you learn to ride a bike as a child, it's not because you're looking for alternative means of commuting. In contrast, say, to the thousands making their stately morning progress to work through Amsterdam, bike riding for a child has a giddy purposelessness, which renders the two-wheeled contraption barely a mode of transport at all. Whereas the adult's machine dutifully conveys its rider from departure point to destination, the child's is a toy that happens to move in a particular direction, but is just as satisfying— probably more so—if it goes around in circles.

In such freewheeling lies an important philosophical question, that of *teleology*. It's the idea that our actions, indeed our lives as a whole, should have a particular aim, a *telos* being a purpose or an end. One of the many factors that separate children from adults is the apparent lack in children of teleological intent; beyond the immediate ambition of scoring a goal or finishing a drawing, they're not trying to get anywhere or achieve anything. They are unburdened as yet with having to direct themselves toward a particular outcome, and this makes riding a bike not just an activity of childhood, but a metaphor for it: wheeling about defines the state of childishness.

Yet from the child's own perspective, learning to ride a bike points rather in the opposite direction, toward being grown up; it takes that childishness and doesn't so much underscore as overcome it. This isn't to imply that, as you start pedaling independently, you suddenly become more focused on the teleological requirements of adult living. Rather, the grown-upness felt by the cycling child constitutes an agreeable sense of mastery, an intimation of the skillfulness that children associate with adults. Insofar as childhood represents the gradual reclamation of the terrain of incompetence that, as a baby, you were stranded in, learning to ride a bike has all the triumphant satisfaction of a sudden land grab.

In this accelerated conquest, the mastery you acquire falls into two baskets. The first is the technical domination of the machine: keeping the handlebars level, not braking too sharply, maintaining pressure on the pedals. By itself, however, that skill would soon wear off—like getting bored with a jigsaw puzzle done several times—and it needs supplementing with the second kind, the mastery of the self. This involves getting your legs to do new things in conjunction with your hands and your eyes and the ability to harness what were otherwise diverse faculties. Initially, because it can't stand up by itself and because it calls for such novel leg and hand movements, the bike threatens to pitch itself and your body into disarray, but like a horse it also gives you the chance to gather all together and turn chaos into order. Once you succeed in getting all these elements to combine, you achieve what never ceases, even when you get older, to amaze: balancing on two thin discs.

Yet the (as it were) overriding quality you need for learning to cycle is something quite at odds with this purposive approach: an embracing of risk. The whole point about learning to ride a bike is that sooner or later the person pushing you has to let go. Without getting too deeply into cycloanalysis, this discloses a pure moment of doubt and faith. In a quite different context it was described by Søren Kierkegaard, the Danish philosopher of the nineteenth century. That context was religion, in which Kierkegaard held that no amount of reasoning can get you to a belief in God, for at some point you've got to leave reason behind and jump—hence a *leap of faith*. Faith is not rational, which doesn't mean it's irrational so much as that it stands beyond reason. (Kierkegaard also says that the opposite of faith is not reason, but sin.) Reason and faith will never be continuous with each other—a deep gulf stands between them. The same logic applies to learning to ride a bike. How so?

To get from being pushed by someone else to riding by oneself requires the leaping of a ravine between two orders of being—from dependence to independence, from security to self-determinism—rather than making a smooth transition from one to the other along a continuous path. As long as your dad jogs beside you with his hand on your back ("Don't let go!"), you won't legitimately be cycling. Sooner or later you've got to take over and jump the forbidding crevasse between the familiar and the strange. You have to embrace what in Kierkegaardian philosophy is the madness of decision, the vertiginous split second when reason must, in the name of action, go into suspense. In this critical instant of changeover, success arises only if you go at a considerable speed, if you seize the challenge of creating your own forward momentum; otherwise the whole thing peters out into failure and shame. As Einstein (whom we'll come to later) put it, when comparing riding a bicycle with living a life, "To keep your balance you have to keep moving!" When at last you do succeed, you sense the exhilaration to be had on the other side, and together with this adrenal rush, those different, novel, contradictory rules press in upon you, rules whereby to stay balanced, you have to hurtle forward, where safety increases with risk.

Altogether, learning to ride a bike gives you, the child, an early taste of what it might mean to be an adult, to be loosed from the swaddling environment of childhood into the challenging freedom of self-direction. Certainly you had been "free" as a child before you could ride a bike, but it was freedom of an untested variety, a backyard rather than open-country version, and—in Kierkegaard's book—not worth so much. It's only when freedom engages with fear and doubt and ignorance that it achieves credibility. That's the point about freedom: it's wild. So unless you face into its staring openness and tame it by subduing it to your will, you become lost inside it, with too many options and no sense of direction. In learning to ride a bike, you apprehend the wide horizon in front of you and realize you have to make something of it—to urge your bike wheels to cut an arc through its undifferentiated, virgin panorama. Very quickly freedom packs down into the obligation of making a decision, and with decision comes the weighty refusal of that option in favor of this, of turning left rather than right.

In tandem (so to speak) with this new, mature sense of freedom that involves making choices comes one of the earliest presentiments of true solitude. With Dad left behind, proud and panting, you're now off on your own, prefiguring the moment many years later when you will leave home. Although you can ride on the handlebars with a friend pumping the pedals, proper cycling means commanding the helm alone and suffering that peculiar silence that goes with riding a bike: you hear the sounds around you, for sure, but these all coalesce to form an auditory tunnel you rush through, pushing them to one side to let you pass. Out in the world, more alive than ever to the whirligig of the background you weave your way through, you paradoxically assume a foundational sense of your interior self, in a way that later will be padded out when you learn to drive a car. You're out there, but alone; swinging through the streets, but solitary; pursuing an itinerary that, despite its teleological purposelessness, its random deviations, adds to where you're going in life.

Insular and isolated though that scene seems, the very fact that you're riding a bicycle, a machine on wheels, reveals at the same time a far larger teleological story, the bike being more than just one invention among others. Not least because it has established itself as a definitive accoutrement of childhood. It is so vivid a component of early memories one forgets how recent an invention the bicycle actually is and that, for all its seeming naturalness and ease of motion, it did indeed take some inventing. For only two hundred years, astonishingly, the bicycle has trundled alongside that other mechanical horse, the train, with which its origins roughly coincide, making a fitting, if somewhat comic, co-emblem of the Industrial Revolution. Why so late? one wonders. Was it because, unlike other wheeled contraptions—farm carts and chariots of war—the bicycle was always destined to be a vehicle for leisure, far down the list of necessities demanding invention? Other than rickshaws, conceivably, little perceptible gain in productivity has been realized by the bicycle since the Penny Farthing first rolled like the coins it was named after into the Victorian age. And whereas a pottery wheel or spinning wheel might be linked to GDP, the bicycle has remained a net undercontributor to the wealth, if not the health, of nations. True, it could now play a part in doing the reverse, in reducing carbon footprints, but it has never really been an agent of unfettered advancement.

Nevertheless about two hundred years ago, and as if human evolution had been fed with steroids, the bicycle overnight multiplied the biped's velocity on foot, and so in its own way represented progress itself, its spokes and shafts resembling the ingeniously repurposed pistons off a dilapidated mill and its personalized locomotion resembling a promise of new forms of empire: you conquer the large landmasses like India by train, and once settled in your foreign plantation, you pootle about by bike. It's not by chance we give the name *revolution* to these massive lurches in history, technological or imperial, for at the center of this word is that which revolves: the wheel itself. Indeed revolution is merely the speeding up of the forward turning of history, the catalyst to an otherwise slow but equally inevitable result. The direction remains the same: the present fades in an instant to become the past, as if time itself were a cyclist leaning into the front wheel, pushing the road beneath behind. From this perspective, the bicycle captures on a human scale what happens in the broad unrolling of historical time. It both represents progress and gives the most tangible sense of time being used up under its wheels. When you learn to ride a bike, you not only go forth in your own development, you echo the very process of history.

But there are reasons for being skeptical about the notion of history rolling forward like a bicycle, along a path of progress. I'm thinking of Walter Benjamin, the German philosopher who wrote specifically about newspaper boys going around on their bicycles, and about the bike races organized for them by the owners of the paper. If you won the race, you might get offered a job in the office, and thus launch a career in journalism. That suggests a simple kind of progress, of course, but on a larger scale Benjamin was more doubtful. Much influenced by Marx—who famously claimed that all history happens twice, the first time as history, the second time as farce—Benjamin was to deepen Marx's thinking, and at the same time change the "revolutionary" metaphor on which Marx himself was so famously to rely. For Marx, revolution, like those steroids above, would give an artificial kick to the otherwise complacent rolling along of world history that favored the rich, and that's why it was to be recommended. Spinning the wheel of history that bit faster would hasten the desired outcome of an equal society.

Benjamin, however, while applauding that outcome, deplored this "progressivist" way of thinking about it. To conceive of history cycling through political revolutions toward ever greater enlightenment or freedom is to fall for a messianic attitude to the world, which secretly hopes that the end of history will come with the arrival of someone or something to save us all—that it will all be better in the long run. To explain his own (yes, revolutionary) theory, he fabricated instead a counterallegory, not of the messiah, but of "the angel of history":

> His face is turned toward the past. Where we perceive a chain of events, he sees one single catastrophe which keeps piling wreckage upon wreckage and hurls it in front of his feet. The angel would like to stay, awaken the dead, and make whole what has been smashed. But a storm is blowing from Paradise; it has got caught in his wings with such violence that the angel can no longer close them. This storm irresistibly propels him into the future to which his back is turned, while the pile of debris before him grows skyward. This storm is what we call progress.

As is clear from the quote, Benjamin was much exercised by what he deemed the myth of progress, and was particularly suspicious of the idea that mechanical innovations—a train or a bicycle, for instance—might represent a staging post on the way to Enlightenment. All too often, "modernity" contained the seeds of its own destruction; by the same token, "progress" constituted an illusion, designed to justify technological advance for the sake of capitalism. The idea of milestones too would have been suspect. The only rebuttal to this myth of progress, the only way of calming this catastrophic storm, would be to take the wheel of history and stick your finger into it, to bring it to a juddering halt and "make whole what has been smashed."

But if there's a wheel at all to stick the finger into, it's because predating the invention of the bicycle by about 6,000 years was the original invention of the wheel itself.

It's a bizarre thought, perhaps, that it took so long to make the link between a wheel and a bike, but no less bizarre than the fact that the wheel itself needed inventing. It implies that the circle, which along with the square and the triangle constitutes one of the most basic shapes we recognize, is not actually natural. Okay, nature might not boast many "perfect circles" as such, but you'd have thought the primary shape of the round, and therefore the wheel, was a given. Did our ancestors never gaze at the full moon, for instance? Perhaps its primary nature was the very problem: the circle hails from a transcendent, perfect, Platonic world, uneasy at being pulled down to earth, construed as a wheel, and being put to such practical use. But once invented— assuming there was such a eureka moment—it became an indispensable agent of human development, because what it embodies more than anything is the miracle of leverage, the idea that little effort can be ratcheted into a lot of result.

You don't need the Green lobby to inform you of the bicycle's remarkable efficiency, of course, and when you're learning to master it, part of the wonder lies in the living proof of that law of leverage: like a swan your upper body remains relatively composed as the ground beneath your ankles flashes by; with just a few contractions of the thigh muscles you pull easily and still farther away from your dad at the margin. As he gets smaller in your vision, you might also intuit the different sensations each of you feels. There he stands, small, static, and satisfied at having launched his young fledgling, while you are feeling the wind on your face at speed, as fast at least as the rush of air when you were pushed on the swings as a toddler. But this difference of perspective implies more than psychological effects, for there's also the theory of relativity in play.

The legendary scientist who invented the theory didn't just talk about cycling as a metaphor for life. There's also a famously delightful photo of him cycling manically, and indeed somewhat childishly, most unlike Paul Rayment and his allegedly humorless creator, J. M. Coetzee. In that childhood scene of learning to ride a bike, the half-serious, half-crazy notion of Einsteinian relativity—the idea that reality varies according to where you're standing—applies rather well. For a start, the difference between yours and your dad's experience suggests no absolute position from which either could definitively say how fast you are going. You have your own perception, your dad has his; both have their merits, but they're not quite the same. At these short distances, of course, those differences will be infinitesimal; to lend them an experiential reality, you'd have to be cycling on Mars, that is, at a sufficient distance away for the realities to begin to measurably diverge. Yet the differences are real. Why so?

When you learn to ride a bike, the park you're cycling in seems to have the quality of a fixed container that your bike crosses through. There's space, in the form of the park, and there's time, in the form of your cycling from one side to the other. In this model, time and space are related but different things: like a knife and a fork, they complement one another, are often thought of together, but they're also discrete. Commonsensical as the model may be, however, it doesn't capture what for Einstein was the truer truth of the situation. Imagine that knife and fork had been soldered together into one distended metal polygon, or, to use the image favored by physicists, picture the park and the sky around you and you on your bicycle as a vast sheet with slight dips or curves in it. Despite it being "one dimension," however, this space-time continuum is profoundly local, so my space-time is always a bit different from yours. This implies your dad's position on the sidelines is complete in itself; his vantage point is somewhat different from yours, but this doesn't make it less authentic. Contrary to what I implied earlier, there's not one objective reality with two discrepant subjective interpretations of it, but two separate, if near-identical realities. The conclusion being that you must be cycling at two speeds simultaneously, and in two worlds, yours and your dad's—as if you had been cloned.

If such is the complexity of the universe at the macro level, it gets echoed on the micro level by the complexity of learning to ride a bike that I've described. It involves mastery of the machine and of the self; a leap of faith into a steep kind of solitude, not to mention the possibility of being knocked off, like Paul Rayment. Once we do get it, however, what's strange is that, like swimming, cycling doesn't need to be learned again. Like most clichés, it's true: you never forget how to ride a bike. It's as if, just as cows have more than one stomach, humans have two memories, one for the mind and one for the muscles—hence "muscle memory." When you get on a bike, even after a long interval, your limbs just know what to do even if your mind has forgotten the last time you rode; the instruction file for cycling remains stored somewhere surprisingly close to the surface of your physical recall. And if cycling can *become* a matter of instinct, instincts, paradoxically, can be learned. One thinks of instincts as reflexes we're born with, but perhaps that's not always the case. It's highly mechanical, but bike riding becomes second nature. Unlike playing the piano or speaking German, which can get pretty rusty over time, bike riding remains pristine, a talent ready to be wheeled out afresh at any moment. There are few things in life you can simply pick up again where you left off, but with a bicycle, no matter how old you are, you can embrace your childhood again. Perhaps Paul Rayment wasn't so foolish after all.

5

Taking Exams

Answer THREE of the following questions. You have THREE
hours.

1. In what sense, if any, does music have meaning?
2. How useful is it to speak of a yin and yang from one
   Imperial Chinese dynasty to another?
3. Is international law based upon the principle of the
   sovereign equality of States?
4. Did the Romans always aim to translate Greek accu-
   rately?
5. Is competition between firms productive?
6. Why did Old and Middle English poets dream, and to
   what effect?
7. Do nations have a claim to self-determination that
   other cultural groups lack?

These are real questions taken from past exam papers for
the position of Prize Fellow of All Souls College, Oxford.
It's a position that I've been lucky enough to hold. It must
rank among the more elite in the academic world, with
benefits proportional to its prestige. These include rooms
in a quadrangle built by Nicholas Hawksmoor, overlook-
ing a sundial designed by Christopher Wren, himself a for-

mer Fellow; the services of a personal scout to bring your pigeon post and to help you on with your gown before dinner; the candlelit dinners themselves, of, say, beef fillet and tarte tatin, followed by a dessert featuring claret from one of the world's finest cellars; a termly wine allowance of one's own; the august company of the globe's academic aristocracy; not to mention seven years of uninterrupted freedom to follow one's intellectual bent.

Also proportional, however, is the process you must submit to in order to get in (assuming you already have, as your table stakes, a First Class degree from a leading university). First comes the supposedly informal interview with the Warden, the head of house, in his Palladian villa attached to the college; no hard questions are posed, and one can get away without venturing aperçus into Homer, Hegel, or Heisenberg, but it's nevertheless a step in the process to be taken seriously. Then comes the exam, or rather exams. Of these there are six, each lasting three hours. Two will be on your specialist subject—English, history, law, etc.—from which the questions above are taken; another two will be general papers on politics, culture, current affairs. The last two are perhaps the most distinctive. The translation paper involves being handed a booklet of up to twenty passages of prose, each in a different language; you are invited to translate as many as you care to, in the time available. You may also request a language in case those offered aren't sufficiently stretching or exotic—Coptic or Basque, for example. The subject of the last, the essay paper, is much thinner altogether. It comprises a single word, this being the title of a subject on which you are to extemporize with the authority and wit of a young Dr. Johnson. Among such words in past papers have been *Illusion, Memory, Discretion*, and *Taste*.

As if these tests weren't testing enough, you are obliged in the course of them to be swept away for a more formal interview in the wood-paneled common room, with twenty or so of the Fellows, gathered in vulturish black gowns, just to keep you on your mettle. You must also attend a cocktail party for you and the other examinees. And if, once your papers have been graded, you are shortlisted for the one or two places offered each year by the College to coincide with the feast of All Souls in November, you meet your final battle. This itself consists of two stages. Summoned to appear on a Saturday afternoon, you are interviewed by the entire Fellowship of the college—seventy Fellows, all leading authorities in their field, many ennobled, a living Who's Who of the intellectual establishment. At the end of an infinite table covered in baize you sit, fielding both direct questions on what you have penned in your exams and curve balls from Fellows trying to see what you're made of. That night, your suit now changed for a tuxedo, you are called back one last time for the climactic dinner, at which your skills in conversation, not to mention your ability to negotiate a battery of silver cutlery and a flight of wine glasses, are placed under the not least exacting examination of all.

For all its Dickensian wonder, all its evocation of another world and indeed another time, the All Souls process only intensifies what is true of all exams, and the paradox at their heart. Namely, that a meritocracy produces an elite. True, few titles could be more glamorous in academic terms than that of Prize Fellow, but nor could the rigor by which the fellowships are awarded be made much stiffer. In fact the former is a consequence of the latter, the very concept of an exam being shaped like a funnel. At the top it opens out with an invitation to all and sundry to try their luck; a sporting spirit prevails. At the bottom it drastically narrows, allowing only a handful of candidates to pass through, thus constricting that spirit for the sake of a small league of the successful. This makes exams both the most and the least democratic mechanism routinely in use. Meritocracy accompanies democracy up to a point and then turns about-face to oppose it.

It's a paradox that exercised Max Weber, the founder of modern sociology. He pointed out that, on the one hand, exams involve a "selection of those who qualify from all social strata rather than a rule by notables. On the other hand, democracy fears that a merit system and educational certificates will result in a privileged 'caste.'" So, if exams play fast and loose with democracy, why endorse them at all? Pierre Bourdieu, the French sociologist, would argue that their main function is to adorn the exam taker with the "symbolic baubles" that make him or her appear to be part of the establishment; it's not really about mental capability but simply about being recognized, rightly or wrongly, by the great and good. And yet, if you're wedded to democracy as equality and don't want to impose a test of any sort on job candidates, you'd have to make sure there are enough positions for everyone. In other words, exams start to become irrelevant only when there's far more work to be done than there are people to do it.

According to a second paradox, however, the crème de la crème produced by the democratic exam systems often finds itself assigned to serving the people, and things come around. Because the origin of the exam system coincided with the need for social administration. At least, this was the case in ancient China, where the exam was first conceived.

A country of that size needed significant administrative capacity, a workforce to manage its affairs, and that meant recruiting according to a newly selective process. In doing so it may have produced that privileged caste, but this process also generated the resources needed by the state to run itself. And so the true origin of the exam lies not in demo- or merito- but bureaucracy. The examination was born, and with it an apparatus that continues without fundamental alteration today, not just in China but in the smaller operations of the French and British Civil Service, for example, who, like exam cheats, copied it. Hence the word *mandarin*.

As well as their paradoxes, such systems, which are focused principally on academic prowess, have more obvious blemishes: they suggest that what you need to run a country are brains rather than anything practical. When a school roof starts leaking or a hospital catches fire, there's not much the policy wonks can do to help. That said, the Chinese approach, based on Confucius, actually placed braininess second to the virtues of self-discipline and disinterested learning. But no less a figure than Plato believed that states should be run by the intelligentsia; his great work of social theory, *The Republic*, explicitly put people into a pecking order, with the clever bureaucrats at the top. But either way, Chinese or Greek, the exam system aimed at producing men who, intellectually and/or morally, were ready to serve. The purpose of exams, therefore, was always clear: to produce the nation's stewards.

Sadly, perhaps, the clarity of that original conception hasn't carried over into modern life, and we're in some confusion as to what exams are for. Today one might legitimately wonder any of the following: Are exams principally a gateway to get through to the next educational stage, regardless of content?

A memory test to see if you were paying attention during lessons? A way of killing time and affording artificial structure to the otherwise amorphous school year, like tasking soldiers with scrubbing the parade ground with toothbrushes? Or just a thinly disguised form of punishment? Do they even provide you with the skills you'll need, or, like requiring a would-be judge to run a marathon, do they require feats of prowess whose relationship to later employment is utterly tenuous? On the subject of exams, it's quite possible that we've kept the practice but lost the purpose.

Or perhaps, to propose a negative definition of meritocracy, the purpose of the exam system is simply to reduce nepotism. Without exams, the elite would merely reproduce itself, hiring the next generation in its own image. (Not that this can't happen anyway.) In which case, exams are the intellectual equivalent of the incest taboo, designed similarly to diversify and thus strengthen the gene pool coming through. Nobody intervenes to pull strings or give a leg up, an abstract principle that becomes intensely palpable when you take your first batch of formal tests at school. Apart from the call on your intellectual faculties, you face the more intimidating challenge of having to perform unaided, for more than anything else what defines being examined is that it can't be delegated; as you take your seat at the desk, nervously lining up pen and ruler, no one can step in on your behalf. In this, taking exams resembles mundane events such as bathing and momentous ones such as circumcision, neither of which lends itself much to outsourcing. Exam taking thus has much in common with being born (not to mention the opposite of being born), an experience of separateness that in the case of exams gets reinforced on results day: there's no swapping your grades.

It's more than just solitariness, however. Slightly different from solitude, closer to loneliness, but most like conscience, the state into which an exam impels you is that of a frank and potentially terrifying look inside yourself. In this dread moment of reckoning, you realize with exceptional keenness how bare or full your mental cupboard really is, how prudently you have been husbanding your resources, and how prepared you are for the task at hand. In effect, an exam gives you incontrovertible data on who you are and how conscientiously you've managed the gift of being you. A tiny heralding of the Last, this first judgment sees through you as you; therefore the cerebral challenge includes an irreducibly moral dimension. Who do you stack up as? When you take away the props, what's left? Are you a person of substance, or someone who's used others to hide behind? Perhaps this helps explain exam nerves; maybe it's not just the test, but having all the other props, like supportive teachers, taken away. No wonder people dream about exams long after they're over: an exam is a trauma, and trauma reappears in dreams.

Scary stuff. At the same time, however, and despite the overwhelming singularity of the experience, the setup is, and for the sake of counternepotism has to remain, entirely anonymous. Even your name gets withheld from the examiner, in case of prejudice, and you're allocated a number. Now completely faceless, you're at that number's mercy. It penetrates far deeper than your name, which it treats with a callous disregard, like a pathetic vestige of personality. When the going gets rough, and even the questions leave you dumbfounded, you can't say "But I'm Robert!" because when it comes to exams, it's purely the content of your answers that counts, regardless of any personality lying behind them. The number maintains its stony-faced impartiality throughout. Of course, this assumes your personality won't leak through to your answers, something easier to achieve in math than in literature, which, being largely an exercise in interpretation, might well reveal an idiosyncratic trace of personal style (not to mention the giveaway of handwriting). Still, the principle of anonymity applies, leaving you like a prisoner stripped not just of the contents of your pockets but even of your patronym. Thus divested, you're then asked in the most probing fashion for an account of your abilities, and yours alone. In short, taking an exam stands as perhaps the most personal but the least personalized experience of your life.

And so the examination begins: "You may turn over your papers." Now you are *invigilated*, where the vigil undertaken ensures no talking, the outer silence of the exam hall contrasting sharply with the mental commotion inside every bowed head. The questions you'd been speculating about unveil themselves at last: predicted, unpredicted, easy, difficult, fair, unfair, or just plain mystifying. Now the clock has started ticking, thus making a pressing reality of the other axis of exam taking: the first axis on the graph being that of how much you know, while this second one plots how much time you've got left in which to display it. It's knowledge against time, a cruel contest not least because it lies in the nature of knowledge to be gathered and to unfold at a creeping, studious pace. The examination scoffs at that, making of knowledge a sport. And because it's a sport, the exam becomes as visceral as it is intellectual, the adrenalin teeming, the heart itself clattering like an alarm clock.

Small wonder that for many the experience can overwhelm; small wonder they resort to cheating. For although we tend to treat cheating as skullduggery, it's more ordinarily a symptom of fear, of the trepidation not unreasonably felt at this moment of trial. Besides, there's a rank order that goes from serious fraud—breaking into the office safe the night before to steal the questions—to the pitiful, amateur ruses that fall short of malfeasance proper. These include writing in a larger than usual cursive to bulk out your paltry knowledge of a subject; hedging your bets in a translation exam by heavily inking in a word; responding to a multiple choice question by selecting two answers where there should be one. Then there are the slightly less forgivable crimes, like writing things inside your cuff, in the folds of a bandage, or on a crib sheet planted in the bathroom for you to consult when nature apparently calls. All count as cheating, to be sure, but they also speak to a fearful optimism in the face of humiliating ignorance.

Most desperate of all, perhaps, must be the direct copying from your neighbor. Conniving, it might look from one perspective, but what makes copying in an exam the archetypal form of cheating is that it's so artless, so ingenuous an expression of one's own inadequacy, such a naked admission that the solitariness won't be borne. It's a moment when you newly appreciate the class nerd you've hitherto disregarded or defamed. There she sits, hair tied back, her body a neat bundle of mental intensity and diligence. The edge of her script peeps out just enough for you to peep back, and you're led into temptation.

It seems like another moral moment, and indeed it is, but copying brings with it questions of an equally philosophical kind. The concept of copying was to underpin much of the thinking of Jacques Derrida, who himself had to hurdle the exam barrier between an upbringing in Algiers and the grandeur of the Grandes Ecoles in Paris, France's most sought-after institutions. Say you're taking a geography test, and you get the question "What is the capital city of Spain?" For the life of you, you can't remember, and so you crane toward the nerd's desk on your left, willing her elbow to stay out of the way. You see from her scrawl that the answer begins with an *M* and, your memory jogged, you write in nervous triumph on your paper the single word *Madrid*. Well, for this fretful scene to take place at all, it must be that the word *Madrid* was copyable, that it wasn't bound to remain on her script. So what?

No matter how many times I write or say it, I can't use up the word *Madrid*. A bottomless resource, the word willingly agrees to be mined ad infinitum. In fact it's precisely because words are copyable—inexhaustibly so—that the examination has to impose strictures to guard against it; if words weren't copyable, that invigilator could go home. Copyability, or what Derrida terms *iterability*, means that even as words are used, part of each word escapes. Every time it's spoken or written, there's a bit of the word that holds back, not getting used up in this particular usage, allowing the word to be used again. To put it in starker terms, every time you write or say a word, that word is present only to the degree it is absent—absent in the sense that it hasn't given itself entirely to the immediate context, but is making itself available for other contexts at other times. Its inexhaustibility means it's never fully present, and the word *Madrid* as written on that girl's paper is supplied with an invisible escape route from itself, a secret tunnel that enabled it to slip away from her paper and let itself be written on your own. Once it's on your script, it's copyable again.

If you buy Derrida's argument, you will see how, because so much of knowledge consists of words, knowledge itself becomes an open resource. Nobody finally owns it: we're merely its caretakers. When it comes to exams, you can never be tested on "your knowledge," just on your ability to temporarily warehouse a modest arsenal of know-how. Indeed the fact that we go on to forget it implies that the knowledge never penetrated deeply enough to define us, and even that knowledge has nothing to do with identity—we just borrow it as and when needed. Filing out of the exam hall for the last time, you'll already have forgotten some of the key data you so urgently revised the night before and that were so fleetingly vital to your future.

When, at last, you are told to put down your pen, all the tension and worry in the buildup can be released. A joyous relief breaks out, the satisfaction at having undergone the test, and (in most cases) never having to go through it again. You've earned your stripes, paid your dues, won your spurs, and can hand the baton on to the next generation. For this end-of-exams jubilation is also an expression of generational rhythms, of passing a milestone in history that the year above had to pass before and that the year below, like new recruits watching the battle-hardened troops come home, will have to pass in turn. Americans speak of a "class of 2011," for example, as an academic proxy for an almost biological stage. Exams make an arch through which more than ephemeral knowledge parades; shared memories, friendships, antagonisms, all press through that narrow space. They create a sense of oneself as part of a troupe, for although they expose one's existential solitude, they're nearly always taken en masse. Perhaps this is what sets exam taking apart from the majority of other milestones in one's life, which tend to be indexed to the progress of the individual exclusively. It's most peculiar, of course, that something so intense and private happens in such large numbers—the academic equivalent of a mass wedding—but it does allow this year's cohort to come together immediately afterward to reflect, process, bemoan, celebrate, and generally unwind.

6

Having Your First Kiss

Apart from your own, I wonder whether the following mightn't be the most memorable first kiss of all time:

ROMEO If I profane with my unworthiest hand
        This holy shrine, the gentle sin is this.
        My lips, two blushing pilgrims, ready stand
        To smooth that rough touch with a tender kiss.
JULIET   Good pilgrim, you do wrong your hand too
           much,
        Which mannerly devotion shows in this;
        For saints have hands that pilgrims' hands do
           touch,
        And palm to palm is holy palmers' kiss.
ROMEO Have not saints lips, and holy palmers too?
JULIET   Ay, pilgrim, lips that they must use in prayer.
ROMEO O, then, dear saint, let lips do what hands do;
        They pray. Grant thou, lest faith turn to despair.
JULIET   Saints do not move, though grant for prayers'
           sake.
ROMEO Then move not, while my prayer's effect I take.

Memorable it may be, but had you been allowed to study Shakespeare's famous lines in, for example, an Eastern Bloc country before the collapse of Communism, your understanding of them would have been entirely different from that of your fellow students in the West. In the United States or the United Kingdom you would have been asked about the emotion produced by Romeo and Juliet's sensuous language, about the richness of its meaning, about the genius of its author. In the USSR or Maoist China, by contrast, your professor would have asked you to set out the sonnet's rhyme scheme (Romeo and Juliet's first exchange forms a perfect sonnet), to enumerate the consonants in each line, and to define the syntactic relationship between each clause. Thus you might have responded that the meter follows a strict iambic pentameter, five beats per line over ten syllables; that the letter *s* features forty-two times and in thirteen of the fourteen lines; and that this proportion represents a more frequent usage of the letter *s* than usual in English. Any venturing into the meaning of the poem, let alone the feeling it evokes, would have been deemed at best irrelevant, at worst degenerate—which is precisely why Shakespeare, whose artistry is so hard to ignore, often fell foul of the Communist censors. An art it may be, but literature should be treated as a science, something whose natural excessiveness, like a wild garden, needs to be brought under control.

The same went for kissing itself, the subject as well as the climax of Romeo and Juliet's tête-à-tête. It is said that the Soviet dictionary of the Russian language defined kissing in purely mechanical terms, as the mutual impacting of the buccal membranes, the increased production of saliva, the activation of certain nerve endings. Any romantic or sexual element to kissing was excluded, the entire act reduced to its functional components. As it happens, there's a number of interesting scientific facts more recently discovered about kissing, such as that our lips have the thinnest layer of skin on the human body; that they contain an unusually high quotient of sensory neurons that fire off impulses to the brain; that kissing may reduce stress; and that, quite unaccountably, kissing couples tilt their heads to the right twice as often as they tilt to the left.

Try telling all that to Romeo and Juliet. Their purple poetry proves a kiss couldn't be further from the factual and the functional. No, a kiss is a matter of delight, of play, of a delicious hide-and-seek, as light as a feather and as solemn as the prayers to which Shakespeare's lovers allude. It hovers like a net to catch all their fluttering feelings: hope, expectation, anxiety, curiosity, relief, abandon. It waits for them teasingly at the end of the sonnet, to bless the miracle of love at first sight. Listening to Romeo and Juliet, one wants to say that above all kissing proves there are more mysterious and wonderful things in the world than are dreamed of by science.

But what's interesting is that this romantic wondrousness finds itself enhanced rather than diminished by the formal elements, the scientific structure, of the verse, and that the young lovers themselves seem more than a little aware of it. That repeated *s*, for example, makes the lines sound like the kissing they describe, especially because the *s* often combines with a *p*, not only in the word *lips* itself, but also *palmers, prayer's,* and *pilgrims.* Each time Romeo or Juliet speaks, he or she repeats at least one key word that the other has just enunciated, as if their fates were becoming laced together through each letter of that word. The final two lines create not only a couplet but a couple: they demonstrate the union and symmetry between the lovebirds. The result is that the supposed polarities of formality and playfulness become braided together, like the lovers, into one: the verse binds their unbounded feelings, and in binding, increases the pleasurable tension; part of their clever joy comes from alluding to such feelings through a very formal language. Thus Romeo and Juliet play with each other's words in a verbal fondling where formality of language parallels and mocks the formality of courting protocol. Before Romeo and Juliet proceed to kissing each other on the mouth, their words kiss. And it's precisely by choosing such words that Romeo and Juliet exhibit the dexterity with their lips that is requisite for the kissing to come, their lips moving with words as if rehearsing the finale of this very stagy encounter. After all, before a first kiss, each lover is to the other mostly a set of words, and so one subconsciously stretches those words as far as possible into mimicking, and thus precipitating, the kissing act they foreshadow. At the same time, both of them, knowing the kiss a certainty, seek to defer it, each phrase both postponing and securing the moment of bliss.

In Shakespeare's account, a kiss is not just spoken about in poetry—a kiss becomes poetry. A sort of literary phrasing, it moves the mouth to make beautiful shapes, shapes like a heart, that attract the other person. When the other comes close, the kiss takes form as a pleasing rhyme between two faces that tenderly meet. The kiss also enjoys that extraordinary poetic combination of the formal and the free, the ceremonious and the sensual, the ritualistic and the romantic. For unlike mowing the lawn or doing the ironing, there's no natural conclusion to kissing, no stage at which there's nothing more to be done. In this it also differs from sex, envisaging no climax, no terminus at which desire is, if only for a moment, switched off. If they didn't have to sleep or eat or visit the bathroom, lovers could and probably would kiss forever.

Unless you're a teenage boy, perhaps. According to gender stereotypes, he can tolerate this open-endedness only so long. Hoping to shunt the kissing-carriage onto the track of foreplay, which would give it a determinate destination, he becomes frustrated if kissing remains stubbornly on the road to infinity, leading nowhere, sweet but as insubstantial as cotton candy. He wants his first kiss to become his last kiss, so he can get on to more serious forms of interfusion. To the stereotypical teenage girl, meanwhile, it might well be that kissing needs no target to aim at. For her, a kiss counts as a kiss even if it leads only to more kisses, each pressing-together a moment of fruition. Perhaps she's content with this deferral precisely because the first kiss presages a first coitus; her readiness to multiply the kisses might be about putting off that sweet but anxious moment of being breached. Kissing speaks, albeit silently, to the beginning of sexuality. In the sonnet, the language of pilgrims and shrines shows, in the gravity running beneath its wittiness, that the holy of holies—Juliet's maidenly innocence—is indeed to be invaded before long. (We already know her parents are keen to marry her off.) A hitherto saintly purity will be given up for a physical, worldly, nonideal sensation. Like the pilgrimage to which Romeo and Juliet refer, it conjures up a mysterious destination, a hazy place of higher and, as it's known, biblical knowledge.

There's a more disquieting ending that this otherwise trivial pastime of kissing summons up, also hinted at by Shakespeare, namely that the first kiss gestures toward death. That's partly because in marking a rite of passage, you have by definition taken another step away from being born and on toward its opposite. For Shakespeare, this spectral quality to kissing, its premonition of death, lies in the reference to the stone-cold statues of saints and in the fatalistic allusion to the mouth as a tomb—the tomb where Romeo and Juliet tragically end up—with the tongue as the body lying still or active within it. Once you kiss someone, you signal something about destiny, "sealing with a kiss." At one level, it's the legitimation of the relationship. After all, a relationship without a kiss, like a marriage without sex, remains unconfirmed. You can argue that your relationship is chaste, that it exists on a higher plane, but the kiss serves like a signature to contract the connection, literally to tighten it. The kiss makes a glue between two people that lasts long after the mouths are dry again. Although we might sleep with more people than we marry, and kiss more than we sleep with, there's no denying the metaphysical as well as physical bond involved in kissing, especially the first. Once bonded in this way, you are saying to your partner that, in principle, you've made a compact that can't easily be undone. Shareable by only two people, it works like a signature or pledge and a secret shared.

Despite being so pregnant with such meaning, in itself kissing remains a strangely hollow activity, a kind of eating without food. Akin to crying, kissing seems to have an inner trigger, but without external benefit. Whereas sex can claim at least the goal of procreation, nothing can be achieved by kissing, and so it becomes its own end. Perhaps that's why kissing is always personal, whereas sex, for good or ill, can be reduced to anonymous transaction (hence "sex workers"). This completeness-in-itself of kissing takes us back to poetry and more generally to art, at least in the theory of Immanuel Kant, who was writing, appropriately perhaps, at the dawn of German Romanticism in the late eighteenth century. Struggling to fit art into the larger scheme of reason, Kant decided it constituted a "purposefulness without purpose," supply sans demand. Think of a painting: it looks beautiful and makes sense on its own terms—it even seems to be saying something—but, apart from the fact that it can be sold for cash, a painting is no real use to anyone. It has the drive of something with purpose without having been called for; essentially gratuitous, it makes up for not being demanded by creating a demand within itself. Well, this definition can do double duty for kissing. Fashioned and imparted as if the greatest intent were involved, each kiss suggests something of import, whereas it's a largely redundant activity. Nothing results from kissing as such; no one asked the lovers to kiss, but having begun, they continue as if with the most pressing task. Like art, kissing is purposefulness without purpose.

Kissing also embodies the Kantian concept of the sublime. Today the word *sublime* describes surpassing beauty or wonder, but originally it carried more ambiguity. The sublime formed a wild zone between human reason and a confrontation with God, that place where logical calculation runs out and one suddenly looks up and apprehends the giant presence of the Lord ahead. As such, the sublime generated at least as much terror as pleasure. It adverted to the risk of losing oneself in the storm of divine intensity, and it's this in particular that pertains to kissing, which leads to a loss of orientation. Your eyes are closed, you're clasped tight against another body, and the more you do it, the more you want it, the appetite both feeding and stimulating itself. It all smacks of madness, an intermission in the daylight, a sublime self-undoing parallel to the Kantian sense. Because you can't kiss and speak at the same time, the kissing tongue replaces the mother tongue altogether. Kissing becomes silence, rational speech cut off, causing us literally to be dumbstruck. We are sublimely frozen, like the petrified figures at Pompeii, into a stupefied position, locked with another person, and this inhibits not just talk but mobility. No wonder Shakespeare makes kissing allude to carved stone.

This setting in stone becomes unignorably evident in the kiss of Auguste Rodin's imposing sculpture—if not as famous as the figures of Romeo and Juliet, then on a par with the couplings of Brancusi, Doisneau, and others. Indeed the kiss in art forms a subgenre of its own, a half-way point, perhaps, between the double portrait and the nude. Although the history of statuary abounds with semi-naked figures and direct eroticism—think of the *Venus de Milo* or *David*—*The Kiss* maintains a startling erotic direct-ness, making for a dramatic impact that seems to operate on a series of contradictions. For a start, there's the sheer private nudity of the bodies being so publicly displayed; then there's the intimacy of their touch contrasted with the super size of the figures, as well as the tension between the tenderness of the contact and the roughness of the marble. Rodin's handicraft is a far cry from the polished stonework of classical Greece. This rusticated stone continues the con-tradictions by taking something essentially fleeting—the kiss—and, like a fossil, making it permanent. Which isn't to say that kisses can't be extended—first kisses soon give way to marathon snogs—but an extended kissing session features numberless individual kisses, pauses, and insatia-ble restarts. Nor should we ignore the basic physical opposition, or rather union, of man and woman. He is far larger than she, and their kiss insists on the asymmetry; when standing, the woman has to go on her tiptoes, the man has to stoop.

But above all—and perhaps this represents the Kantian sublime better than anything—the two lovers seem at once undeniably human and impressively godly. As if kissing indeed opened a channel between the earthly and the divine, Rodin's lovers, especially the woman, seem on the point of transport. A kiss might seal, but it also heralds an opening or unlocking, a reaching into a new dimension, theological, mythical, or plain fanciful. From kissing a frog to kissing the stone at the tower of Blarney Castle in Ireland (said to bestow on its supplicants the gift of the gab), the courage needed to make this trusting contact brings disproportionate rewards. Not unlike losing your virginity (see the next chapter), the kiss provides a key to a hitherto guessed-at but unknown realm, a secret garden of delights. Why the fairy-tale quality to kisses? Well, if magic did exist, it probably would make use of kissing: both play on the margin between substance and substancelessness. A kiss disappears in the having of it, each tiny oral plosion a puff of smoke. And because kissing marks the first meaningful use of the lips since suckling in infancy, it retains something whimsical, nostalgic, and imaginary. Yes, kissing can be undertaken with much gravity and deliberation, but an untutored joy conditions it, as if every kiss were stolen in a tree house, furtive, joyful, and somehow made up. It's real, and the evidence offers itself to the taste, and yet it's unreal. Kissing doesn't quite belong in the world; even in the midst of an extended, physical clinch, the two lovers, so present to each other's bodies, will also exist elsewhere.

To indicate that the sexuality of kissing was prefigured in infant life is of course to make a psychoanalytic claim. The British analyst Adam Phillips describes kissing as follows: Because as babies we use the mouth to siphon milk from the mother's breast, the two functions of nourishment and pleasure merge as one. You could even argue that the fact that these two haven't yet split off from each other defines infancy: taking pleasure through the mouth and taking food through the same orifice can't be told apart. It's only with the waking of sexual feelings that we come to isolate erotic gratification from the basic needs of sustenance.

So far so good. But there's a catch. In those infant years we learned that our pleasure depends on an *object*, that is, another body. At first, this other body is that of the mother, but as she weans us, her body fades into the background, leaving us with the wish to replace it. Because we're still some way from puberty, however—the era when one begins to seek independent bodies that aren't our mother—we replace the mother with ourselves. We go from feeding at the mother's breast to wanting to feed on ourselves, and in the process develop narcissism, or self-love. Unfortunately, however—or fortunately, depending how you look at it— we cannot kiss ourselves. We can press against the cold and unrewarding surface of the mirror, but this only makes more acute the chronic pang of loss that we must endure until we find another proper object for the lips to kiss.

Phillips dwells on the grotesque image of the mouth kissing itself, and there are other peculiarities in this psychoanalytic interpretation. Most obviously, our first kiss works to repair a loss, that of the mother's breast when she stopped breast-feeding. Or, to take the alternative theory of Desmond Morris, the zoological anthropologist, it might be that kissing has its origins in primate mothers chewing food as a means of predigesting it for their offspring. As the mother passes the masticated bolus to her baby, the two mouths come into contact, meaning that kissing might feel good because of an ancient link with sustenance. Either way, as much as a first kiss marks a step forward on a journey, it also refers back to that point of plenitude in our past, as if it were a physical nostalgia. Which suggests that the first kiss is never our first, but always our third. The first was that period in the arms of the mother; the second was that failed attempt at self-kissing. And so if the third kiss—that is, the first grown-up kiss—brings relief, it's because it *sublates*, both reprises and transcends, the experience of the first two. It's not that you're kissing your mother or yourself, but that a trace of these experiences remains, adding a historical depth to that rapturous moment on the dance floor or behind the shed, when you first join your lips to another's in an explicitly amatory fashion. It might feel as though the whole world converges on you and your kissing mate at that point in time; it might even feel as though all time has been wiped out. But beneath that kiss are autobiographical layers that reach back in time to your first days on earth.

From this point onward the mouth redefines itself. Although gratification comes with kissing—as indeed with the oral sex that might be the next milestone to which it points—this is gratification as something more luxurious than the meeting of needs. Just as one's taste for food starts to become more sophisticated, hunger slaking becoming less important relative to taste, so the mouth searches out more refined forms of pleasure. And if your kiss is accompanied by stirrings of love, your mouth will also seek out new words—the modern-day version of Romeo and

Juliet's sonnet—adequate to the delight of the experience you are feeling, words that are themselves then pleasurable to speak. So although we might think of infants as being the mouth-centered ones, we find in adult life all sorts of ways to sustain and diversify the pleasure the mouth can bring. Although we can't talk while we kiss, kissing eventually speaks volumes.

7

Losing Your Virginity

When Madonna broke onto the global pop scene with "Like a Virgin," her supremely superficial song belied a peculiar depth. Here was a highly sexed woman named after the mother of Christ singing about virginity—something she'd clearly lost some while before—thus evoking, deliberately or not, the great Christian fable of parthenogenesis, otherwise known as the virgin birth, while with her own uninhibited sexuality mocking it. That Madonna Ciccone herself hailed from a family of devout practitioners only made it curiouser. The song's vapidity might have pointed elsewhere, but for anyone who cared to consider them, the ironies were rich.

This splitting-off into levity and mythic depth captures well the ambivalence in our modern attitudes to losing one's virginity. On the one hand, not losing your virginity provides matter for mirth, even for outright comedy, as in the film *The 40-Year-Old Virgin* or the doggerel *Four and Twenty Virgins*, designed to provoke puerile sniggers all round. Why funny? Not only because virginity concerns sex, but because it concerns the anxiety about sex. Partly there's something a little pitiful, naïve, or vulnerable about those people who've still to cross the river of initiation; we feel a bit superior to them, and on the far shore they seem small. And partly there's the relief that we ourselves have swum to the near side more or less unscathed. Losing one's virginity means gaining wider acceptance.

For those young adults on the cusp of losing it, however, that free-floating anxiety easily coagulates into genuine apprehension, bringing on a host of concerns, from the physical to the emotional. Will I be any good? Is this the right person? Will it hurt? Consult any agony aunt for teens, and you'll see the same misgivings perennially aired. Here's a recent example from an online newspaper:

1. If you don't trust your partner to respect your wishes if you change your mind about anything, you should not be having sex.
2. You can't get your virginity back once it's gone, so make sure that you are having sex for the right reasons. Emotional blackmail, such as "You would if you loved me," or peer pressure, such as "Everyone else is doing it," are not appropriate motivations for becoming sexually active.

Sex might be fun, but the pious officiousness of such warnings has the not only unintended but also unhelpful consequence of making something already challenging all the more daunting. Although it's perhaps the ultimate bodily experience, one in which reason finally gets put aside in the name of intimacy and pleasure, first-time sex should, according to these elders, be approached with all one's cognitive faculties on red alert. Thankfully, most teenagers don't listen to too much advice. If they did, the world might stop turning.

The solemnity carries through, or is perhaps generated

by, the religion with which Madonna the artiste has so singular a relationship. One could describe Catholicism as a cult of virginity, but for all the intrigue that suggests, virginity itself was merely a solution to a theological conundrum. No sooner do you sign up to the notion of God becoming man, than you have to account for how he actually arrived on earth. If you say he's born exclusively of mortals, he can't be born of God, and, less defensibly still, he becomes the product of sexual intercourse, which hardly seems appropriate. And if you hold that he simply lands on earth like a meteor, then he's not really God made man—he's just a god (as it were). The only option left is the one on which that cult was founded: the logical contradiction of a virgin birth. That's the only way to square the circle of a god becoming human.

But far from being the distortion of logic it so plainly seems, the idea of the virgin birth should be read as genuinely mysterious, and along with the wonder of Christ's apparition, the thousands of paintings of the Madonna and Child manufactured in the Renaissance celebrate this triumph of sublimity over sense, rapture over reason. The blue cloth traditionally donned by Mary in those depictions thus works as a veil between the two realms, as if she's saying "Behind this technically ludicrous construct lies a deeper truth." With the contradiction surpassed or at least suppressed, Baby Jesus can be as plump and fleshy (in Italian art) or as rigid and wizened (in German) as the artist fancies.

Take the most famous of all madonnas, Leonardo da Vinci's *Virgin of the Rocks.* In a grotto of jutting rocks, Mary sits with Christ at her feet; he is blessing a young John the Baptist, while the Angel Uriel looks on. Like many in its genre, the painting seems to express an infinite love on the part of the mother for her son. Indeed to the German philosopher G. W. F. Hegel such images enable us to appreciate spiritual love in its purest form. The love between a mother and son already enjoys a special cachet, and the virginity of Mary, her sexual innocence, concentrates that love all the more, for no sexual moment has interfered, by way of conception, to overhumanize and thus diminish it. Most important, it was Mary's virginity that for Hegel made it possible for the divine spirit to manifest itself. For him, the whole world was made up of spirit, but unless it was literally brought down to earth, that spirit would remain merely ideal. Mary's virginity therefore offers the perfect channel for the spirit to enter the world: it can arrive on earth and achieve reality without compromising its pureness. Hegel had found a different route around the self-contradiction of the virgin birth, for in giving birth to Christ, Mary was giving birth to the spirit of the world.

Hegel's view can be taken further. As the title *Virgin of the Rocks* suggests, it's not the infant messiah but Mary herself who takes pride of place, her body forming the dead center of the canvas and her luminous face its apex. However, while this compositional arrangement establishes her importance and brings her forward in the frame, she also recedes. As much as she is the central figure, she is merely the background to the momentous scene around her skirts, where the first meeting between Christ and John takes place. This suggests that her innocence, her virginity, is what allows other things to happen, just as her body had been used a short time before to allow the birth of Christ. As she had been the empty vessel exploited by God as a surrogate mother, so her innocence marks a withdrawal that permits Christ to come forward. For the sake of the mystery of a God becoming flesh, Mary effaces herself. In other words, her virginity provides a form of self-sacrifice. It says, "I make myself small, so that you may be great." According to this logic, to lose your virginity is to sacrifice the possibility of sacrifice.

It's probably this self-sacrifice that motivates the celibacy of nuns. Losing one's virginity would not only defile the body or distract from prayer, but preclude their offering themselves up in such holy fashion. (The word *sacrifice* means "making sacred.") Of course, nuns are particular targets for those juvenile jokes and sexual innuendo, and for all the aforementioned reasons. But the virginity of nuns, because elective and because geared toward soliciting religious mystery, retains a venerable quality that, like their bodies, demands a deference over and above the humor. It's mostly the same for monks, except that because they are males, their virginity, or at least their celibacy (you can become celibate, whereas you can never become a virgin) more bespeaks the mastering of the self, the dousing with cold water of the flames of desire.

Common to both nuns and monks, and creating an undercurrent beneath all our notions of virginity and the importance of not losing it, runs a nostalgia for previous innocence that harks right back to the Garden of Eden. By keeping yourself pure, you're aligning yourself with that prelapsarian world, holding the corruptions of the flesh at arm's length. There's even in this gesture of self-preservation a tacit wager that if you don't dip into the fleshpots, you might remain immortal, as would our celestial ancestors, Adam and Eve, had they not succumbed to temptation. That makes innocence a play at eternity. Something of this otherworldly ideal survives in pubescent girls' talk of "saving themselves," and their mothers' advice to do so. The ideal includes the fantasy that time itself might stand still, keeping one's life as intact and as empty of incident as the original sin-free garden.

If I speak of girls rather than boys, it's because, despite gender differences becoming elided in other ways, when it comes to virginity it's still different for girls. As our agony aunt was implying, the loss of a girl's virginity can amount to a loss of respect, such that nothing less than her moral worth hangs in the balance. Where the same loss for a boy equals a gain in street cred, for a girl the forfeit will usually be more ponderous. Why so? No doubt those religious myths of innocence play their subliminal part. Less intangible is the brute fact that it's the girl who risks getting pregnant. There are also evolutionary reasons for females being more circumspect about giving up their flower: being pregnant without a mate brings with it a real sense of vulnerability not experienced by the male impregnator, who can still run around and save himself, if need be. Not to mention the chemical difference whereby females are endowed with the greater share of the chemical associated with long-term pair bonding, oxytocin. Its presence suggests that, for girls, losing virginity means not just having sex, or even getting pregnant, but an expectation of embarking on or committing to a relationship.

On top of all that, there's the perforation of the hymen. Whereas for a boy, losing his virginity might leave an emotional but no bodily trace, for a girl there's the possibility of being found out. Virginity tests continue in parts of the world out of not just anthropological interest. It's rumored that before pledging her troth to Prince Charles,

Lady Diana Spencer herself—as if marrying into the Royal Family weren't sufficient ordeal—was subjected to such an examination. Surprisingly perhaps, the hymen has been the focus of a different sort of examination altogether: the philosophical. Jacques Derrida (who helped us with cheating in the chapter on exams) was himself much obsessed with veils like the blue cloth worn by Mother Mary. He interpreted the hymen as a special case of this barrier between the outer world and the inner sanctum. According to Derrida, who refers in turn to Friedrich Nietzsche, there is throughout the history of Western thought a metaphorical association between woman and truth, neither of which was self-evident, neither of which revealed itself instantly, neither of which was immediately intelligible. Made enigmatic by a veil or a hymen placed in front of them, both the truth and the woman demanded the subtlest ploys by men to penetrate their meaning. Apart from its physiological function, the hymen serves to heighten the mystery of what lies behind it, as though sexual seduction were a means of encroaching upon the holy ground, whereupon true knowledge might be obtained.

Highfalutin as that may sound, Derrida is only tapping into a vast seam of thought that has been mined since the Greeks. A good example of this connection between virginity and mystical truth would be the Parthenon in Athens. As in the *parthenogenesis* I mentioned at the beginning of this chapter, the word *Parthenon* means "virgin" and is the soubriquet for the chaste goddess Athena, after whom the city was named. The building, of course, was a temple, made up of inner and outer chambers, with access to the most sacred parts hidden behind a veil, forbidden. In this sense, the temple became the architectural form of the goddess's body—the temple was she. Think too of the later vestal virgins in Rome, whose job it was to guard the fire burning in the deepest recesses of the temple (hence, incidentally, Swan Vestas matches, which refer to that fire). In all cases, the virgin not only protects her own virginity, keeping her body *virgo intacta*, but also guards a rare truth, meant only for the trusted. Put that into psychological terms, and it's as if the motive for the girl's greater reticence over surrendering her virginity might be connected to the feeling that she's allowing her boyfriend to access what's truest about her.

Derrida characterizes the hymen "as protective screen, the jewel box of virginity, the vaginal partition, the fine, invisible veil which, in front of the hystera [the uterus], stands between the inside and the outside of a woman, and consequently between desire and fulfillment. It is neither desire nor pleasure but in between the two." If the hymen stands before the truth, it also stands before, or in the way of, a blissful satisfaction. But what is such sexual bliss made of? Why, despite all the caveats, the risk of pregnancy, the anxiety, and the fear of squandering a sacred truth, do teenagers so fixate on this rite of passage? The anticipated pleasure must be pretty great to outweigh all those other disadvantages. So what's the attraction?

At one level, the desire to have sex and lose one's virginity in the process resembles the desire to walk that I talked about earlier. Regardless of peer pressure, you are programmed, biologically, to advance through this stage of life, even if walking might appear to be the more essential. Those who fail to lose their virginity attest generally to a want not of desire but of opportunity. Which means that *desire* might be the wrong word for the teenage intent involved in losing one's cherry: it's something less in our control. Okay, there are a few more decisions involved, but it's a natural process that you'd have to try hard to avoid.

This natural process has a disquieting underside. On becoming sexually active you become both more and less useful to the species. More, because you're able to make babies and so keep the species going; less, because by conjuring up the next generation, having your first sex declares that your own obsolescence has been set in motion. If you're capable of sex you're in theory capable of being survived by your progeny, and so although losing your virginity might feel like the beginning of a great sexual journey, it's also the beginning of the end.

At first it looks as though Sigmund Freud, the ultimate thinker of sexuality and early fantasy, wants to counter this reading of sex as the harbinger of death. He calls the desire for sex *Eros* and against it pits a deathly nemesis called *Thanatos*. Where Eros is all about libido, contact with others, growth and change, Thanatos looks coldly on all those good things and strives to destroy them. Like Order and Chaos, Eros and Thanatos are set up as the metaphysical pillars between which the whole drama of life gets played out. And so we enact a tug of war between these contrary forces of expansion and contraction. We throw ourselves into our work, but then pack it all in; fall desperately in love, but then shrink back into ourselves; and so on.

But as Freud's thinking develops, so the boundary between Eros and Thanatos begins to fray, and they end up behaving alike. He notices that the aim of our sexual desire, paradoxically, is its removal: so long as we desire sex, we carry on in a state of frustrated agitation, and for Freud, such agitation is precisely what the ego can least tolerate. We'd much rather have a quiet life, but, just as paradoxically, in removing agitation we sink back into a state of inert contentment that's barely distinguishable from death. Not orgasm itself, but the calm that succeeds it was our goal, and this quietus promises a deathly stillness that motivated us all along. Eros comes to look suspiciously like the Thanatos it started out opposing.

All of which means that losing one's virginity might be a way of stating two things. First, there is the need, felt acutely by hormonally supercharged teenagers, to quell the sexual agitation that courses through them, to satisfy it and so bring some respite from the unresting provocations. It's not easy being a teenager, at the mercy of your libido, and sex is both the cause of and the answer to the disturbance it creates. Second, losing your virginity and achieving temporary fulfillment restore on a local scale the state of inertia that prevailed even before the sexual partners were born and cast out into this mottled terrain of partially requited desire. For Freud, the longing for sex, which can barely be told apart from the longing for death, aims at getting back to the state of ultimate simplicity that prevailed long ago, before human beings evolved into the complex creatures they became. If life is unbearable, it's not just that our desires keep pricking at us, it's that we've become so mightily overdeveloped that we'd prefer to reverse through evolution to become single-cell organisms again. The calm that arrives with sexual satisfaction provides a muted, but highly prized, encore of that primal state, and so the path toward losing one's virginity curves backward to the origin of the species.

I have given teenagers top billing in this chapter, along with an assumption that first-time sex will be premarital, and thus an experience or experiment largely unconnected to the wider bonds of responsibility. Though losing one's virginity retains a great deal of its gravity, it's probable that few Western teenagers expect their first lover to be their last. Yet only a couple of generations have elapsed since losing one's virginity was equated with getting married and the phrase *wedding night* a euphemism for sexual initiation. It's a theme taken up by Ian McEwan in his 2007 novella, *On Chesil Beach.* Set in England in 1962—the year, according to the sardonic British poet Philip Larkin, before sexual intercourse began—McEwan's story sees Edward and Florence checking into a seaside hotel on the night of their nuptials. Both are seized with apprehension, she because she's dreading the moment of being "entered," he because he's so keyed up for this long-anticipated moment.

The result is premature ejaculation followed by shame followed by recrimination followed by the marriage's annulment. It's a tragedy not just because the newlyweds genuinely loved one another but because 1962 marks the last year, as Larkin implied, of the nineteenth century, making it impossible for them to openly discuss what's transpired and make reparations. Both are victims of their era, and their very marriage is sacrificed to this anachronistic prudishness that does nobody any good. Partly because of that long Christian history, with its idolatry of Mary, virginity had become a matter for reverential hush or ecclesiastical earnestness, neither of which makes a particularly good bedfellow on a wedding night. And so if, by contrast, Madonna Ciccone managed twenty years later to bring being like a virgin center stage, we probably owe her some thanks.

8

Passing Your Driving Test

To understand the cultural differences between countries, one could do worse than compare the guidance on driving. Take the instructions on hand signals as illustrated in the California Department of Motor Vehicles guidebook versus the UK Highway Code. In the latter, a tiny figure pokes a nervous hand out of a sensible royal-blue hatchback to make a right turn. In the California version, the car is a long, cool, canary-colored convertible, and the man driving extends his arm insouciantly from a flame-red short-sleeved shirt into the Pacific air. Almost everything you need to know about the two cultures lives in those pictures.

But even in the UK a little bit of that American expansiveness spills over into the driving culture. When British teens apply for their test, they've got in mind more than acquiring the technical competence to operate a machine on four wheels. Like young adults around the world, they're envisaging expansive horizons unfolding up ahead of them. It's not the driving that matters in passing the driving test, it's the potential—which makes the driving license a cousin of the passport it mimics, and makes every first car, no matter how crappy, a yellow open-top cruise-mobile.

The sentiment is captured well in the title of an essay by Andrew O'Hagan in the *London Review of Books:* "A Car of One's Own." Where, in prelicense days, one was taxied around by one's parents or consigned to schlepping about on public transport—reliant in both cases on other people—the prospect of being able to drive sketches out a rosy vista of independence. Passing your test marks a moment that looks both ways: over your shoulder, back to the cutting of the umbilical cord, and forward to the road ahead, to getting your first apartment. (O'Hagan's essay alludes of course to the more famous *A Room of One's Own* by Virginia Woolf.) The car offers its newly licensed occupants a space for expressing themselves without interference from society. Rules of the road there may be, but compared with the exhilaration of having other rules left on the pavement—the rules of being told what to do at school, home, or work—they are trifling. One's car is one's castle, each driver a despot of the dashboard who can arrange things just so, turn the wheel according to whim, and directly influence his or her own destiny.

Like Virginia Woolf's room, the car stands as metaphor for the mind and its free associations, a careering cave of self-exploration: while the car may traverse geography, the mental ground covered also counts. To pass one's driving test, therefore, is to be let into a world where one explores deep inside the self and looks out through the windshield from the interior of the car in the same way one spies out of the cranium through the eyes. If it's true that "you are what you drive," it's equally true that driving makes you most yourself, conducive as it is to a state of contemplation or introspection quite at odds with the grating and churning of traffic up ahead.

Scrawling on the suffragist wall of the early twentieth century, Woolf believed women ought, like their male counterparts, to enjoy access to the clubs, the libraries, and the dining rooms where thought could relax; they too needed the chance to find their vocation, and so the "room of one's own" became both euphemism and slogan for female emancipation, calling for a space other than the kitchen to dominate. As such, Woolf's ideas inspired generations of women and provided the deep background for many a feminist work, including the 1989 film that adopts the traditionally male form of a road movie, and then inverts it. I'm referring to Ridley Scott's *Thelma and Louise*, starring Susan Sarandon and Geena Davis, an inspired annexing of this preeminently macho genre and the recasting of it as the quest for justice for women, a movie that en route questions the province of cars as lying exclusively in the world of men.

The odyssey embarked on by the eponymous heroines is literally triggered when Louise shoots dead a man attempting to rape her friend Thelma. As the duo flee the scene of the crime, to become unintentionally mired in further trouble that's increasingly difficult to reverse out of, driving becomes an exploration not just of the self, but of the self as undeniably gendered. It's impossible for humans to live in neutral, in both senses, the film wants to say. Though victims, Thelma and Louise get treated, because they are women, as criminals, as fugitives from the law that Louise herself, by opening fire on her friend's assailant, had been hoping to enforce. Whereas for men, driving promises freedom, for the women it turns into a process of creeping self-incarceration. The farther they drive, the guiltier they become, suggesting that passing your driving test might come with different connotations for men and women. The very fact that cars are so associated with men creates an unjustified suspicion of women in the driving seat.

Carjacking the male road movie on behalf of females, Thelma and Louise thus expose our assumptions about life at the wheel, and although they ultimately fail to overturn them, they at least get a taste of the freedom of the highway hitherto denied, like the gentleman's Bourbon they sip along the way. Until they run out of road, that is. The story comes to a head at the top of a cliff, their green 1966 Ford Thunderbird (itself a classic boy's toy) beetling above the vertiginous drop of the Grand Canyon. The very landscape forms a mythic symbol of the gaucho penetration into the final frontier, not to mention its association with the other movie genre that *Thelma and Louise* reinterprets: the spaghetti western. The car might have replaced the horse, but the confrontation with the Wild West is just as primal, the stakes just as high. Cut off by a line of police vehicles that demarcate what could be the OK Corral, the women, faced with a life behind bars or worse, put the pedal to the metal and hurtle over the edge.

That link between horse and car is important, and not just because the horse-drawn carriage anticipated the car, nor because of that lineage of road movies in spaghetti westerns, nor even because horse riding has been as much associated with men as has driving a motor vehicle—something we're reminded of by the word *chivalry*, which refers to being an adept horseman, and the Spanish word for gentleman being *caballero*, meaning "horse rider." If it was at the beginning of the twentieth century that the substitution of the horse with the car began in earnest (disregarding the Ford Mustang, which aspired to combine the two), this period coincided, without coincidence, with that of the Modernism which Virginia Woolf came so much to represent. Ostensibly an artistic and literary movement,

Modernism harbored a fascination with the cars, airplanes, and other machines it developed alongside. Is that peculiar? Not at all; both, after all, were modern.

In those newfangled artifacts, however, Modernism saw a vision of the future that was notably bifocal. Through one lens, there was apocalypse. Here was the car outperforming mankind and threatening to flay it of its humanity, and the more reactionary voices of the age condemned this so-called triumph of the machine as the harbinger of (C)armageddon. Such predictions were not entirely inaccurate. Before long Henry T. Ford launched a new era in manufacturing with the mass-produced automobile, which, while advertising freedom for all, enslaved those who had to build it. Pretty soon the car was a byword for large-scale manufacturing, and *modernity* meant not thronging with the avant-garde but pursuing the rationalization that would inexorably replace human beings with the robots they were in any case becoming.

Through the other lens, however, the car, along with the airplane, seemed to announce the human being's belated arrival at its godlike potential. Modernist artists like Filippo Tommaso Marinetti and Jacob Epstein created sculptures and drawings in which human beings got spliced with ultratechnological functions and were reborn as angels of speed. In this interpretation, learning to drive meant access to an earthly divinity. Under this exhilarating reign of the machine, humans would drill through to untouched strata of experience, wherein lay the key connection with Modernism as an aesthetic movement: the thrill of speed was a new experience of beauty. One of the most iconic paintings of the period, a 1925 self-portrait by Tamara de Lempicka, portrays an It Girl in a sea-green sports car—the precursor of Thelma's Thunderbird—with cheekbones as smoothly grooved as the hood of the sleekly powerful machine she so suavely masters. A zoom of one's own, the car functions as an extension of its female driver's cool, detached will. She is sexy, calculating, and in control. Car and human merge in a gesture of nonchalant supremacy.

And so the car altered, for good and ill, conceptions of what it meant to be human—both a dehumanized unit of production and a superhuman agent of self-overcoming. A similar bifurcation occurred in the fate of the car itself. For the mass market, the car declined into another labor-saving device, scarcely more glamorous than a washing machine. At the same time it established itself as an aesthetic *objet* in its own right, admired not only by the Modernist cognoscenti, but by aspirational consumers for whom passing the driving test led to putting the car one drove on display, like a piece of art. Even the engine, especially that of a Mercedes-Benz or Rolls Royce, could be considered a thing of aesthetic merit. Now a car might be functional and beautiful at the same time, like a well-made scythe, the irony being that cars boasted about overcoming such agrarian living. The very distinction between form and function was thus surpassed, the two soldered into one aerodynamic line. Look on the website for, say, the Aston Martin DB9, and you'll see the same advanced logic played out today. It's the mixture of performance and pleasure that counts, an integrated experience that makes it hard to resist. Setting aside that this was James Bond's car, and the sexism that implies—cars, like ships, are still referred to as female— here is a machine whose lines both appear and disappear, are both prominent and subtle, existing at a kind of vanishing point that coincides with its potential speed.

In fact it's with Romanticism as well as Modernism that driving has a great deal in common, and this helps to explain the poetic power of passing your test. The word *romantic* has come to denote sentimentality between lovers, but it began with the idea of a quest, the word referring to a setting-forth. In medieval literature *romance* signaled less a love story than an adventure that would be aimed, most critically, at finding the Holy Grail. This isn't to say it didn't contain the "romantic" motifs that would later come to dominate the genre; its most celebrated emblem was the eminent knight Sir Lancelot, sallying out from the court of King Arthur on his trusty steed and thereby winning the heart of Lady Guinevere. Note again the horse as prototype car and the horseman as courtly gentleman, but focus on the fact that both glory and the lady that is its emblem can't be found at home. To achieve success you have to venture out, and that involves transportation. When the romantic knight gallops forth across the drawbridge to go in quest of heroism and win the maiden, he's anticipating the young man of today passing his driving test in order to make his mark on the world and get the girl.

Not that this "romantic" aspect to driving always involves the petitioning of a beloved. In its masculinist form, it can be enough to cut loose. Take Jack Kerouac's thoughts in *On the Road*, a novel that, for all its modernity, belongs squarely in that tradition of the quest: "What is that feeling when you're driving away from people and they recede on the plain til you see their specks dispersing?—it's the too-huge world vaulting us, and it's good-by. But we lean forward to the next crazy venture beneath the skies."

The skies expand and there's no doubt that driving means encompassing this larger dimension that leaves others behind. The "crazy venture" thus nurses a virulent strain of anarchism, a "Fuck you" mentality empowered by the driver's ability to arrogantly accelerate out of a situation rather than face the music. While the driving test emphasizes what a responsibility it is to be at the wheel of an automobile, it's the off-ramp leading away from responsibility that lends driving its appeal. It's not long before you're staring less at the dials than at the badlands imagined beyond the ripple of heat haze up ahead. Of course, this ability to evade moral capture is based not on the driver's own derring-do, but the rather humbler fact that a car packs a horsepower enabling that driver to get away fast—much faster than he or she could on horseback or on foot. If this is moral freedom, it's fuel-injected.

Nor is this flight away from normal society all fireworks: it also induces loneliness, the absence of connection and relationship. The car has always been more about leaving than arriving, everyone a speck disappearing from everyone else. This driving off into the sunset that comes with passing your test therefore points to *negative liberty*, the idea that you're free so long as other people don't bother you. The concept is associated with Isaiah Berlin, the Riga-born philosopher and raconteur who helped a twentieth century spooked by totalitarianism to conceive liberty anew. But negative liberty is, as the name suggests, only the first base. It comes about through the mere removal of constraint, and beyond the need to obey basic rules of the road, that's what happens when you pass your driving test. It offers up the too-huge world rather than something specific, removing problems rather than creating solutions. You multiply your options when you pass your test, and that can actually be onerous. "Negative" in a double sense, negative liberty has little to recommend it.

Positive liberty, on the other hand, brings some responsibility, as it puts the onus on you to make the most of your life. It means identifying opportunities and venturing out to realize them in a not unromantic way. Driving is an interesting case in point because it provides a literal vehicle for doing just that; passing your test means access to a new world of personal fulfillment. And yet the effect of this positive liberty is . . . traffic. If everyone's venturing out, that adventure into the new you quickly gets stuck in gridlock. It sounds deflating, but if traffic is the consequence of too many cars with competing interests, the very fact that they're competing means each car will be pursuing its own itinerary. In other words, traffic is the result of individual freedom. If, say, the totalitarian states Berlin was so appalled by were to actually prescribe who drives where and when, the problem of traffic would summarily be solved; the car system would operate like a train system, according to a centralized schedule that would moderate collision and congestion. Cars, by contrast, are animated by the individual will of their drivers, and in this sense the traffic to which they contribute represents their positive liberty. In principle, they move freely, even if in fact their progress can falter. The next time you're stuck in a traffic jam, you can console yourself, therefore, that the inability to move has been caused by its opposite: the permission to do so.

So much for positive and negative liberty. There's also the just-as-equivocal type of liberty—nothing to do with Isaiah Berlin—that we experience when actually learning to drive, in the form of the dual-control car. You carry on as if operations were in your own hands, but should you mess up, the instructor's foot hovers over the second brake, ready to save you both. This masterful backup works not like the totalitarian but like the liberal state: it conjures the illusion that you're setting your own direction of travel, while reserving the power to call you to a halt at any moment. Call it *false liberty*, if you like. It continues after you've finished taking driving lessons, the reason being that you pass your driving test only once you've internalized your instructor's instructions. In other words, you've learned to control yourself and thus comply with the rules without the corrective presence of the instructor. In political terms, you've become a good citizen who requires minimal monitoring, precisely because the rules of good behavior have now been transferred to you. This is liberty that works by replicating its rules among its citizen drivers.

This sense of false liberty is then paralleled in the simple mechanical difference between automatic and manual transmission and what they lead to. The technological advances in car manufacturing being what they are, these days there's far less driving involved in driving. Parking assist, lane-departure warning, cruise control, and even thermal recognition of pedestrians who'd otherwise proceed at the mercy of your swerving into them—all these innovations manifest in technological form an invisible driving instructor ready to compensate for your all-too-human errors. Driving a car becomes ever more like monitoring the autopilot on a plane, and "learning to drive" starts to sound pretty easy.

And so you cruise on, cosseted in your technology-enabled car, padded in a cocoon of safety. As long as you don't crash, that is. The driving instructor's second brake isn't there just for instruction—it's a matter of life and death. After all, to be *romantic*, the journey out has to involve risks, be they the dragons of medieval myths or the sheer danger of the speed achieved by Modernist machines. Of these the ultimate must be Donald Campbell's *Bluebird*, the 400 mph supercar of 1967, again celebrated as much for its aesthetic as its aerodynamic prowess, but the cause of Campbell's inevitable death. Behind such kamikaze excess lies the idea of "live fast, die young," and the car crash as a perversely glamorous symbol of untamed youth. Think of Campbell's American near-contemporary, James Dean, killed while letting rip in his Porsche 550 Spyder, or the more philosophical example of Albert Camus, who also died in a car crash, and for whom the desolate reaches for racing through would have held special significance. If there's one philosophy more than another that might be associated with driving, it would be his. Like those evacuated dustbowl landscapes of the spaghetti western, Camus perceived the world as a dry wasteland in which man (yes, it's a highly gendered genre) can choose to be overwhelmed by the featurelessness or, on the contrary, make his mark upon it. The car thus becomes an instrument of both literal and metaphorical self-direction, and passing your test means gaining access to this inner capability. The danger, in this sense, lies not in the environment beyond the car's interior but the lack of courage within. The only thing to fear is oneself, and if you can overcome that, then volition and action may at last coincide. The authoritarian precepts you had randomly to obey are slipped like chocks under the wheels, and you now switch on the ignition with an intent to drive into your own particularity, to penetrate through the outer crusts of unfreedom that have been clad about you, to find and release that inner genie that has been dancing mutely within you for years.

Given this trunk-load of associations, taking your driving test can never be just about obtaining permission for driving. It's always about achieving higher levels of self-realization, far beyond the necessities of living. The same goes for cars themselves, which long ago surpassed their core target of conveying passengers between two points. Cars get faster as average road speeds slow down, to become not just a metaphor for a room of one's own, but that room itself. A car is now a somewhat mobile lounge where you can listen to music in air-conditioned comfort while your passengers watch TV, adjust the lumbar support on your seat while turning down the heat it emits, and toggle the interior lighting while your GPS guides you into the nearest parking space. Driving might be going on during all this, but it's barely more than background. Which means that the ultimate aim of learning the mechanics of driving is to be able to forget them, allowing you to cruise in comfort toward your destiny.

9

Casting Your First Vote

In my neighborhood, on opposite sides of the street, stand two cafés. One has plastic chairs and serves greasy breakfasts to working men, while the other, which has leather sofas, is actually a *caffè*. The extra *f* is supposed to make you think it's genuinely Italian, even though the staff are Polish. In this establishment you are not restricted, as you are on the less sunny side of the street, to tea and coffee. No, here you can purchase cappuccino, espresso, double espresso, dry coffee (with very little milk), shots of flavoring, hot milk frothed for babies and sold as "babyccino," not to mention infinite varieties of tea and tisane. In short, you have a choice. Set aside the research that shows most people order the same drink every day and that more than three options creates confusion and even irritation in the chooser: choice must be intrinsically good. It belongs with a larger democratic project that gives people options. The extra *f* must stand for *freedom*.

But is democracy, and the concept of choice on which it's based, all it's cracked up to be? George Orwell said, "In the case of a word like democracy, not only is there no agreed definition, but the attempt to make one is resisted from all sides." The reasons are many. A free vote tends to the middle, and the average of all voters will usually be fairly unremarkable. Unlike countries ruled by militia, say, which generate authentically hostile opposition, democracy tends to reduce the difference between political parties. What begins as choice produces a lack of it, because most people prefer something fair to middling. That can be particularly demoralizing when casting your first vote: all those inchoate thoughts about society must now be funneled into selecting one or two names from parties whose agenda matches your own only up to a point.

Then there's the disabling sense that a single vote won't make any difference. Of course, reason dictates that every vote counts, and the result of an election is nothing other than the sum of each individual will. And yet when you're at the polling station, your vote looks so flimsy. Even the very next vote popped into the ballot box could immediately cancel out your own. We think democracy a triumph of Western thinking, but the problems don't end there. Is democracy a means or an end, for example? Especially when the West engages with non-Western countries, it's as if democracy is the answer to everything, as though nothing happens once a government has been voted in. And is democracy the best way of running a country or merely the least bad? We don't like authoritarian regimes, for sure, but democracy can lead to insipid policies and consensus-based decisions that are no decisions at all. Finally, should everyone have a right to vote, or should there be some eligibility criteria to do with intelligence, say, or experience?

On top of all those old chestnuts to do with voting and democracy, there's also a set of more philosophical issues. Take the ballot box. While the ballot box is all about secrecy, about protecting the identity of the voter, democracy springs from the very opposite, that is, refusing to leave matters in the shady corridors of power and insisting on hauling them into the open. Allegedly the transition from monarchy or feudalism to democracy is precisely this progression from darkness to light, from the subfusc decisions announced by the few to the daylight choices made by the many. Power, or at least the say over who's in power, gets spread out to the wider population. And yet to protect the identity of those who vote, these daylight choices have to be placed in the darkness of the black box. Even where the actual receptacle is see-through, the voting papers are still folded over to hide who has voted for whom, thus preserving anonymity; if they weren't, those voters, like witnesses at a Mafia trial, might find themselves at risk of reprisal. A free and fair vote, which includes everyone and which no obscurity should cloud, nevertheless establishes and protects a mystery at its center, of who has voted for whom, and is symbolized in that black box. The transparency on which democracy depends, depends in turn on secrets; it is the withheld knowledge that permits the unfettered practice of democracy.

Then there's the matter of trust: this transparency so vaunted by democracies is said to build it. Compared with those that are rigged, one can have faith in such free and fair elections, and certainly they're preferable to the alternatives. Trust is an effect of transparency, and so long as you can see that the electoral process was aboveboard, you've no cause to doubt the result. You might, however, have cause to think again. For if trust has to rely on transparency, it isn't trust in its true sense, but a form of "seeing is believing." What could be more straightforward than trusting what's transparent? It's there before your very eyes, which is one reason for making the ballot boxes in Britain out of Plexiglas; it's so easy that there's no need to trust at all. Genuine trust, by contrast, begins where transparency ends: at exactly the point where less than everything is visible and you have to have faith in what can't be seen. The irony, in other words, is that monarchy and feudalism require higher levels of trust, even if this creates a heightened risk of potential abuse. Democracy, by contrast, actually reduces the need for trust, placing its citizens in the position of monitoring those in power rather than letting them get on with the job.

Finally, democracy is potentially antidemocratic. Within certain limits—voters must be both adult and *compos mentis*—democracy aims to be entirely inclusive. But because it decrees that everyone can have his or her say, this inclusiveness is obliged to include views that are not just liberal or conservative, but antipathetic to democracy per se. Where we might imagine that anyone in his or her right mind would vote for a Western system, authentic democracy involves the possible success of communism, fascism, and totalitarianism, ideologies that wouldn't hesitate to dismantle the democratic apparatus that put them into power. By welcoming difference, democracy has to put itself in jeopardy. As a state of affairs it's bizarre, even if it puts trust back into the equation. More bizarre still is the fact that in being implicitly invited to say "I'm different," each voter has the potential to exclude himself or herself from the inclusivity at large. What democracy encompasses is a set of individuals any of whom could represent an exemption. The grand act of social participation that is voting depends on being an individual, with all the separateness that implies.

Thankfully, perhaps, when you cast your first vote, such contradictions are unlikely to come to the fore. Although you might have weighed up the candidates' pros and cons, and the choice might have led you to reflect on democracy's all-too-obvious limitations—that not one of those candidates can meet all our aspirations, for example—it's the novel feel of the maiden voyage to the polling station that will be the more salient. Not so far behind that of registering a birth, death, or marriage, the experience of first-time voting is easily profounder than most other civic duties, a rite of passage that launches you irrevocably into the new territory of adulthood. While drinking, sex, and driving (not simultaneously) are all capable of bestowing grown-upness, there's nothing quite like voting to make you feel that the outside world now takes you seriously. The difference being that those other transitions are mainly hedonist; in theory one can drink and have sex responsibly, but in practice such pursuits fall well within the realm of personal pleasure. What's more, they're subjective, whereas voting transplants you into the objective world, positions you as part of the *demos*, or citizenry, and so suggests that the responsibility you have is to others. Despite that strange logic of exemption that tangles the roots of the democratic ideal, walking up to the voting booth carries with it this sense of being part of a larger whole. Yes, you vote privately and according to your own conscience, but always as a contribution to the larger count, despite that insidious feeling that your vote won't make any difference; you are smaller than the whole of which you are necessarily a part, and so there is an implicit acknowledgment of that very *demos*. And you're hoping to elect people who will run it, implying that between you, the next administration, and the state it administers, you accept a link.

Not that voting can't be self-interested, but even the most selfish self understands that it shares the election with every other self that is enfranchised. Besides, first-time voters, being younger and more idealistic and having less to lose than their stablemates at the polling stalls, tend to vote with a greater social conscience and a more ardent sense of the common good. For this reason it's they alone, perhaps, who should get the vote; often with age, as we know, comes self-protection, cynicism, and small-mindedness. Imagine a world based exclusively on the wishes of first-time voters: earnest, impecunious, and as poorly organized as they, it would nevertheless be militantly honest, passionately creative, and almost certainly beautiful.

Bathetic, maybe, but this prospect of a nation's fate determined by eighteen-year-olds raises a serious point. The contrast between the idealism of the first-time voter and the realism of his or her elder counterpart parallels that between voting for broad ideologies and voting for narrow policies, which in turn evokes a distinction stretching back to St. Paul, between the spirit and the letter of the law (which I'll come to later). While politicians prefer to beat the latest policy drum—an adjusted tax rate, the initiative on road building, reform of the education system—it's less the policies, or even the aggregate of them, that capture the first-time voter's imagination. Whereas the jaded voter might get pretty exercised by the new levy on property, the rookie is more likely to be looking for what lies behind this or that proposal: its ethos, along with the integrity of those doing the proposing.

More critically, the first-time voter is searching for something in that general set of qualities that will help define his or her own, which makes voting a matter less of ideology than identity. A first vote might add bravely to the common pile, but it's equally a private attestation to yourself of who you are. Just as in your earlier teens you might have declared yourself musically an Emo, Goth, or skater dude, so when the time to vote arrives, you establish politically whom you mean to be. It's not irreversible, because you can always change your politics further down the line, but it fixes at a point in time something about you that's never before been fixed, and if you do come later on to alter your political views, doing so will emit the teeniest whiff of betrayal—of the person you once, as evidenced by your voter's registration card, indisputably were. In this sense, the first vote marks a milestone different from, say, passing your driving test or being born, both of which will happen only once. The votes you cast over the course of your life, whether they change or remain the same, contain an implicit narrative of who you are and aren't becoming.

To some it's lamentable, but that notion of an ethos underlying particular policies has got undoably elided with that of the *brand*. Left or right, the party canvassing for your vote must now market itself in such a way that its deepest convictions are brought up to the surface, buffed and polished. Ethos becomes logo. For the American political theorist Frederic Jameson, such practices fit with a wider project of postmodernization. But it's less about the bringing-out of what was hidden, and more a thorough reworking of the relationship between depth and superficies, leaving us with catchphrases that confidently allude to profounder beliefs without ever quite putting them on the table. It becomes enough to cite the campaign slogan to get an ovation—the detail is irrelevant. And it's irrelevant because what changes societies is perhaps rather superficial after all: the mere energy that the slogan can release, no matter how jejune it is. As a politician all I need to say is "Society is broken" or "It's time for change," because these mantras concentrate enough power in themselves to provoke action in the real world. The point isn't that politicians trying to win your vote are full of hot air—that is, all rhetoric without substance. It's that rhetoric and substance, ethos and brand, coincide in a new postmodern fusion where all the depth gets spread across a surface beneath which lies nothing. And although young adults, those voting for the first time, make up the generation born among just such postmodern prevarications, they're the least likely to swallow them. Why does the marketing of politics to first-time voters often backfire? Because (a) those young adults are constitutionally wary of branding, especially in politics: they've been brought up on too much of it in commercial settings like shops and TV advertising not to be alive to the much-rehearsed techniques; and (b) the attempts by old politicians to ingratiate themselves with young voters, no matter how cunningly disguised by advertisers, is usually embarrassing.

This suggests that for all the postmodernization, brand remains very different from ethos, and the young can be surprisingly traditional in favoring the latter over the former. For ethos is tone, feeling, spirit—all those things that are more than the sum of the policies being promoted. After all, policies will turn into laws, and it's the spirit of the laws that will count more than their textual incarnation. As a phrase, *spirit of the laws* refers to Montesquieu, the aristocratic French eighteenth-century thinker, although, as I mentioned, St. Paul stands behind him at the source. In distinguishing between the spirit (*pneuma*) and the letter (*gramme*) of the law—the difference between the intended meaning and how that meaning gets bureaucratically transcribed—Paul was hoping to raise his reader's sights above a narrow interpretation of the early laws of the Christian Church that his legacy was to overshadow. By the same token, casting a vote should be about choosing the right ethos and spirit, over and above any specific piece of policy or legislation proposed in a given party's manifesto. Democracy is a spiritual affair, implying that despite all the manifestos, we do, and perhaps should, still vote with our hearts and not our heads.

And we have Montesquieu largely to thank. His famous tract *The Spirit of the Laws* was to become a touchstone document in the beginnings of democracy, first in Europe and later in America. If not *post*modernization, democracy represents the more basic modernization of just those feudal and monarchic systems that kept the populace enslaved. Although Montesquieu wasn't opposed to monarchy per se, he was passionately against the despotism into which monarchy could, if unchecked, descend. In a sense his work can be read as the fear of the fear that despotism could bring about. By extension, the *spirit of the law* was the spirit that resisted such rule by terror. The key to keeping this spirit alive was therefore a set of internal checks and balances on power. Even kings and queens, who on the one hand represent the ancien régime of monarchism, can, when included in this accountability structure, become part of the democratic process.

Underpinning that process was an administrative function that, if only because the laity staffed it, was already an embodiment of the people. It wasn't voted for as such, but its very basis was incipiently democratic and began to open up the running of the state to what Montesquieu termed *the commons*. Not quite the active voice of the people, the commons was at least a recognition that the sovereign is not the be-all and end-all and that decision making might involve more ordinary constituents. It's not a system of universal suffrage but without Montesquieu it's questionable how much voting would be going on at all today.

Democracy as we'd recognize it now takes another century or so to bed in, and, as they say, the rest is history. Or is it? In talking like this—in relating such grand narratives of the emergence from slavery to democracy—we should perhaps be chary. The narrative itself stems largely from the Enlightenment, which supposedly lay the foundations for modernity, and of which Montesquieu himself was such a luminary. As the name suggests, the Enlightenment thought of history, in an echo of God rescuing the cosmos from darkness, as the gradual dispersal of shadows: just as we evolve from feudal to fair societies, so we advance from religion to science, from barbarism to civilization, and so on. The vote, in this sense, becomes a highly potent symbol of human development, and in casting your vote you're hymning along with the wider praise of that advance.

The up-to-date version of this narrative has to include democracy's defeat of Communism in and around 1989, making voting an implicit gesture of thumbing one's nose at formerly formidable Soviet powers. For a honeymoon period it seemed to mark an apparently definitive happy ending to world politics: no more wars, no more ideology, just plain democratic-capitalist sailing. But it was soon spoiled when, but a generation later, democracy came under attack by the recidivist forces of religious fundamentalism; these, at least in their militantly Islamist manifestations, prided themselves on being expressly antidemocratic. Far from democracy testifying to classical honor, the reverse was true to its new opponents: democracy led to self-interest, consumerism, immoderation, ill discipline, and a general lack of humility.

Because it so coldly upbraided the view that democracy and peace would forever prevail, the events of 9/11, in addition to the multiple deaths sustained, brought on massive trauma and led directly to peace's opposite, the "war" on terror—for which read "the imperative to reassert democratic principles." The Western discourse of freedom thereby interpreted 9/11 not in fact as a correction of its beliefs, but as an aberration, a blip on the course to the all the more ineluctable victory of democracy the world over. According to this view, casting your first vote began to take on new meaning: in the West, it was not just a rite of passage for the individual but a principled restatement of nationalist pride; in those countries still trying to establish democratic systems, such as South Africa, it became a rite of passage for the nations themselves.

The narrative as I've condensed it, at least up until 9/11, has been associated with Francis Fukuyama, the Japanese American Reaganite whose own association with the American neocon movement of the late twentieth century provides one reason for that chariness: it's not a neutral narrative, but politically motivated. At least this was the leftist response, more or less. That is, the United States has an interest in propagating democracies around the world, not just out of amour propre, but so as to create trading partners through whom it can leverage its economic might—the point being that a market needs democracy to make it properly free. Don't be deceived, therefore, that democracy has much to do with an individual having his or her say, because what matters is not your political opinion, but your being licensed to operate as an economic agent and thus augment the wealth of the nation. As you put one hand in the ballot box, the other has been invisibly tied.

No sooner had Fukuyama published his claims for democracy being the buffer at which the train of history would come to rest, and that we'd more or less arrived, than he was practically booted off board himself. Not just philosophers, but historians and sociologists knew only too well that history was nothing if not the history of change, and so to announce what Fukuyama called "the end of history" amounted to a contradiction in terms: the train had merely pulled into a station on a much longer and much more zigzaggy journey. So much so that it led some, particularly in France, to reassert that, barring acts of God, history would and could never end; that it is affected by a principle of chance, making it inherently unpredictable; and that the likelihood of nothing ever coming to disturb democracy's reign was minimal. In this alternative view, *voting* represents not a transcendent human right, but the provisional emblem of a particular moment in history.

It's hard to imagine, but one day we might look back on democracy less as the climax of reason applied to society, and merely as one step in a grander narrative. In the meantime, it retains its fundamental value as the voice of the people speaking. And as a rite of passage, casting your first vote still confers a new sense of legitimacy. No doubt it's absurdly arbitrary that the day before your eighteenth birthday you're a child, and the day after you're an adult entitled to vote. But just because it's arbitrary doesn't make it meaningless. Along with your first sexual experiences, leaving school, and passing your driving test, this casting of the first vote nudges you toward adulthood. However you look at it, you're now a grown-up, and that means you can speak for yourself.

10

Getting a Job

A coal mine—those that are left—will have seams at different depths, including Deep Hard, Deep Soft, and Waterloo. In such names there's something poetic, but the reality couldn't be harsher, and *the coalface* has come to stand for anything in the world of work that's brutally real. Compared with venturing down a mineshaft, is anything more representative of getting a real job? In an era before so many people worked in service industries, mining was perhaps work's very essence. Imagine you're a banker, a real estate agent, or a sales assistant in a department store, greeting a miner just come up from the mine shaft and telling him you're "really stressed." It just wouldn't wash.

A simplistic picture, for sure, but there was a time according to legend when *getting a job* signified exactly the sort of thing we associate with miners. For a fleeting period, when you were an adult-in-waiting, you experienced childhood; then suddenly, at the age of twelve or fourteen, you were sent to follow your dad into the depths of the earth to fetch up the black stuff. Unless, that is, you were a lass, in which case you'd do your best to look useful around the house, holding on for the moment at the village dance when the nice young lad with a job down t' pit would ask you to be his, and the whole thing, in every sense, would reproduce.

For either sex, the boy's getting a job was the fulcrum on which society would pivot and procreate.

This gender dimension to becoming employed and thus economically active is only one of many, but it's key; as the '90s disco hit so unflinchingly put it, there's "no romance without finance." In the stereotype, the girl needs a guy who has a job, which means a guy needs a job to get a girl. You'd think that after a century of female emancipation things might be different, and mostly they are, but such unwritten gender laws don't thaw so fast. For a young man, getting a first job might still produce a sense of male pride, as if he's picturing himself as a potential provider. For a young woman, no matter how careerist, both the possibility of falling pregnant and the actuality of having children create a notably different relationship to work that might mean depending on a man at some point to bring home the bacon.

The greater social change, perhaps, has been to the ideal of following in one's father's footsteps. If there's a pathos to coal mining, it's partly to do with that male tradition whereby father and son would work shoulder to shoulder hewing out the black gold. Getting a job called for little career counseling because what you were to do was given. Although it seemed to apply mainly to trades in which young men would become apprenticed—blacksmith, carpenter, brewer, and even circus performer—the professions enjoyed mini-dynasties of their own: doctors who were sons of doctors, lawyers of lawyers, and so on. Today, however, following one's parents seems almost a failure of imagination; besides, it's clouded by nepotism. Getting a job should mean deserving it, not having it handed to you on a plate.

In all this, I'm picturing the world described by D. H. Lawrence, the English writer of the late nineteenth and early twentieth century, who grew up in the mining area near Nottingham and whose writings explore the tension between the grim reality of such a life and the romantic attempts at transcending it. The very fact that he became a writer is a case in point. Even if it chimed with his mother's upwardly mobile aspirations for her son, choosing such a path was, from the gritty masculine perspective, not just to fail at securing a proper job, but to succumb to effeminacy. What's more, because writing meant rising above the context in which Lawrence grew up and looking back on his experiences with a lofty literariness, some saw it as snobbery; when the writing exposed the sexual practices of the working class, it was seen as filth. Even if it revealed something of animal beauty, the fact that in Lawrence's novels working people got undressed and had sex felt like a betrayal of their work ethic, which espoused modesty, simplicity, and labor, old Protestant values. Getting a job meant confirming one's virtue, and so jobs like mining, which produced palpable sweat, thereby demonstrated the goodness of one's soul; writing, by contrast, might be the devil's work.

And yet writing can't be that reprehensible if only because it's a vocation; unless you plan on producing copy for a newspaper or PR firm, you won't ever apply to be a writer. Virtue-wise it might fall short, but it can be grouped with other "callings," like becoming a nun or a priest. For such people, getting a job is irrelevant because the job has already got them: they become sculptors or hermits in the service of a higher compulsion that felt futile to resist. Something deep inside met with an outer, often spiritual demand, and destiny took over; if that suggests vocations must always be rarefied, consider that such earthly professions as teaching, nursing, and midwifery are staffed with plenty who nevertheless find in them a higher calling of their own. Across the particular careers, the factor common to a vocation is the abandoning of the self to a force that relegates getting a job into a lower division of work.

Effectively that casts every vocation as a job for life. Even actors who spend their days bussing tables or bashing the phone in telemarketing will feel their true métier remains inviolate. The wrinkle on the argument is that the value ascribed to the job for life, once positive, has flipped; where formerly it shouted strength of character—loyalty, tenacity, professionalism, respect—it now whispers of a shortage of creativity and ambition. It's a cruel reversal, but perhaps there are still exceptions: those artists, writers, and priests will maintain a job for life and still warrant respect. But where does this company of higher beings leave everyone else? Are those who merely get a job less welcome in their rarefied world?

Au contraire. For Hannah Arendt, at least, getting a job meant jumping into the maelstrom of work and thereby realizing one's *human condition*, this being the title of the 1958 publication for which she's most remembered. Timeless in theme, its date is not, however, insignificant; brought up in a secular Jewish family, Arendt was all too sensitive to the brutalities meted out to the human being during the war of the previous decade. Her writing carries a redemptive dignity, a tone of salvation, where part of the redemption lies in work.

Less exercised by the distinction between work and vocation than that between work and labor, Arendt saw in the latter an analogue with the relationship between human and animal. An animal merely labors—by foraging food for its family—with a productivity that pursues no outcome beyond survival. Once you're fed, your work is done. The capacity for work, by contrast, defines the human species as such. Though work can include elements of labor—we too have families to feed—it's merely the platform for work proper, in which we fulfill our human potential. So Arendt talks about the progression from the *animal laborans*, the laboring animal, to *Homo faber*, the man who makes things. Whereas *animal laborans* finds matter for its own immediate, mainly food-related usage—a blackbird stretches out a worm from the soil, a bear snatches a salmon from a stream—*Homo faber* has the capacity to make things that have more than use value, things that can be put aside for later and exchanged.

It doesn't end there, for the exchange brings *Homo faber* into contact with other people, thus developing a public realm. Work furnishes the setting in which mankind reaches its highest purpose, which is the constructing of relationships and the very reverse of the hostilities of wartime. Interestingly Arendt uses the same terms to consider works of art. After all, these are never simply used, or at least never used up in their use. And though they can be exchanged, "if they enter the exchange market, they can only be arbitrarily priced." That artworks can be exchanged doesn't mean they're properly exchangeable, because unlike cheese or candles they are not commodities, and boast instead what Arendt calls a *uselessness*—the least use, but the highest standing. What artists like Lawrence produce retains a value beyond value.

In sum, getting a job makes you human by virtue of

connecting you with the goods and services that you'll more or less directly need to sell, and therefore with those who hope to trade with you, all based on the human ability to make things that can be held back from immediate use and taken to market. Arendt wishes it went further, and that having made these mercantile connections with other people, our political nature would get drawn out and we'd become actively engaged citizens jointly fashioning future society. But doing business isn't a bad first step. Her focus on exchange gives hope, and in it Arendt draws heavily on the founder of modern economics, Adam Smith, whom she quotes thus: "Nobody ever saw a dog make a fair and deliberate exchange of one bone for another with another dog." Only humans are capable of such strategic investments and negotiations, and again it's what elevates them above the animals. Rather than devouring it on the spot, exchanging the loaf of bread you've baked speaks to a far-sightedness that only humans possess. It lifts them above mere being, with the implication that getting a job conveys you that bit further on the ascent toward affirming yourself as a member of the higher species.

Coming from Adam Smith, however, that was a possibly surprising quote. If there's one thing for which the eighteenth-century Scotsman is known, it's his metaphor of the market's "invisible hand," and yet the quotation implies that, unlike dogs, human beings engage in deliberate acts of exchange with one other, so that any hint of abstract manipulation, such as that of an invisible hand, seems off-key. In any case, there's no entering the job market at all if the demand isn't there, and one definition of a troubled economy might be something as straightforward as "an excess of labor supply." Yet such macroeconomic factors are only the sum of the millions of smaller transactions on the ground. It's easy to mystify the invisible hand as a spirit floating over the market, like God over the waters, but an excess of labor supply arises simply because, on a given main street, there's not sufficient work to go around, and that's because shoppers aren't shopping. In this account, there's no *macro* scene, just a proliferation of *micro* scenarios. If getting a job proves to be a challenge, it's due less to fatalistic economic cycles than the simple fact that the owner of the carpet retailer in your town doesn't need any more carpet layers like you. In his waving goodbye to you, the hand of the market is demoralizingly visible.

With the advent of *behavioral economics*, however, a newly evolved invisible hand has been imagined, whereby such nebulous phenomena as "the mood of the nation" not only respond to but influence the economic conditions on those same streets. (The very distinction between cause and effect fades away.) Characterized less by a hand than a hormone, the market is prone to alarming mood swings, so that getting a job depends on whether not only the interviewer, but the nation, has had a good day. Which sounds utterly disempowering, for these really are factors beyond the individual job-seeker's influence. But it doesn't mean becoming resigned to them. After all, we have governments—massive, accredited institutions that can operate on behalf of job seekers in toto—so surely they ought to intervene? When the market is down, shouldn't they, like a psychiatrist administering antidepressants, provide a fix? Shouldn't they do something, if only because they can?

The problem, according to the behavioral economists, is that humans behave more emotionally than rationally, making any intervention a fairly speculative act. When governments do intervene, however—by tweaking the cost of borrowing, say, or printing money—they create a hand at the macro level that has the advantage of being visible, a wheeze you'd think Adam Smith might smile on. If, that is, the *invisible* part wasn't more important than the *hand* part: the point of the invisible hand was that the market does its own regulation—*as if* there were an invisible hand, not because of one—so the state shouldn't have to.

The market, in other words, is as impersonal and efficient in orchestrating an economy of work as natural selection is in creating an ecology of species. The best thing, therefore, is to sit back and let it happen. Standing in its way might even pervert the order of things, an order that, as natural selection generates health, inexorably generates wealth. According to this philosophy, those who get jobs are those who should thrive, and vice versa; those who don't should "get on their bike" and either find jobs elsewhere or, better still, improvise new ones. The phrase belongs to one of Margaret Thatcher's former ministers, Norman Tebbit, and the sentiment explains why Adam Smith became such a mascot of the free-market economics favored by the Right. But like many appropriations of historical figures—Nietzsche by Nazis, for example, or Machiavelli by misanthropes—it has reduced Smith to caricature. Such compassionless conservatism is not something he would have approved of; he was in any case well aware that, despite the internal gyroscope keeping them buoyant, markets can still plunge. Committed to the humane values of civilization that characterized his time, he had an instinctive wariness of the savagery and disillusion that could result if at such crises governments didn't step in, and he'd hardly join the quasi-eugenicist chorus of the modern hard Right. Which isn't to suggest he'd advocate a commodious welfare state; in modern terms, he might be more of the "hand up, not hand out" school: you still need to get a job.

These days we've more clinical cause for compassion. Boom or bust, we know worklessness to be a leading indicator for mental health problems such as depression, and so if only to prevent later spending on benefits, governments have an interest, when it comes to employment, in keeping levels up. Conversely, and as Arendt was implying, getting a job delivers far more than monetary reward; it bestows a sense of purpose and of oneself as valuable to others. To this extent, "full employment" is as much a moral as a political imperative; on the individual level, getting a job can mean becoming a useful citizen. And though it's on political grounds that China, for example, has at moments claimed full employment for its workforce—leading to the invention of such less-than-vital tasks as shepherding pedestrians over road crossings—those shepherds no doubt benefit from not being penned in at home.

Clearly, working is good for morale. The trouble is that precisely because of those Smithian forces, jobs aren't always as easy to come by as they might once have been in China, and so getting one requires some competing. Hence an obligatory process that, after the desultory trawl through websites and classifieds, kicks off with an application form. Apart from your patience, the form, with its boxes too big for this answer and too small for that, aims to test whether, beyond the legal stuff about visas and criminal records and health, you've got any skeletons in the closet. What exactly were you doing those months after leaving school? When you say "gap year in South East Asia," were you perfecting your Vietnamese, researching the culture for an article, and puzzling out the future of its bilateral relations? Or did you spend your days drugged out on a beach with some transients from Melbourne?

In trying to fill in the gaps about your employment history, what the application form really wants to know is something it can't directly ask. Namely, who you are. Yes, it can help build a picture of your career and can thereby allow the employer to make some guesses about your personality type. However, as an instrument for revealing the essential you, it's blunt. Hence, in turn, the similarly unavoidable interview, which, for all the formulaic questions, comes down to a phenomenon called "chemistry." It's a word we use as if it were a metaphor, but hiring people might literally be a matter of pheromones. Officious types in HR will still take their seats to ensure the job gets awarded on a basket of "competences," "benchmarks," and "skill sets"—of lists that can be ticked—but the person calling the shots will above all want a feel for the pale and nervous character perched on the chair that's always either too hard or too soft. Does this candidate bore me? Engage me? Scare me? No doubt such reactions will be entirely subjective, but then again, much of being at work involves getting on with folk, and chemistry constitutes at once the crudest and subtlest litmus test that can be applied. The interview is thus a case of what in animal psychology is known as "ritual sniffing."

Not that those formulaic questions are so easily parried. One of the oddest things about an interview is that the stock questions—like "Why do you want this job?"—actually do get asked. Both interviewer and interviewee might know such questions are coming as surely as Christmas, but the foreknowledge fails to result in any shared sense of recognition or irony or humor. Why? To share the joke would be to breach the boundary that sets interviewer and interviewee apart and that makes an interview an interview. And so the predictability of predictable questions does little to lessen their intensity. You might have rehearsed your answer a thousand times, and yet you can always be foxed. Or, just as bad, you give your answer by rote, leaving your interrogators looking for the human being behind the automaton you've suddenly become. And even if you can get the tone right, there's the content of what you say. For many things will be straightforward: "I want the job because my whole adult life I've been training to be an architect." For others, however, being completely honest can be inappropriate. "Why do I want this job?" "Because I've got debts I need to pay." "Because anything's got to be better than the dead-end employment I'm stuck in at the moment." "Because my wife responded to the job ad and I'm here to humor her." Getting a job is one thing; getting a job for the right reasons is another.

So how to get yourself to a point where you're finally interviewing for the dream position? I shall end with an insight adapted from James Collins and Jerry Porras, the American management writers best known for a textbook about visionary organizations called *Built to Last.* Having gone on to research the difference between good and great companies, they conclude that the latter derive their greatness from getting three factors to coincide: being good at something, liking doing that something, and having that something bought by customers. You can picture the theory as a Venn diagram in which you want each circle to overlap with the other circles in equal amounts. More pertinently, you can apply the theory to looking for a job.

For example, I might have a yen for bell ringing and rank among the world's leading campanologists, but my income from this lofty profession will never chime with my outgoings on rent. Either I find a way of monetizing my passion, or I go back to the drawing board.

Needless to say, striking the perfect balance of all three factors can be elusive. What's interesting is that during our working lives we'll favor different circles in the Venn diagram in different phases. That student job waiting tables is designed to earn money, and it might even be a bit of fun, but it was never intended to be a vocation. In your middle years you're still focused on earning a paycheck, but are now more oriented around what you're good at—you'll probably have some qualifications—even though the work might still not be quite your passion. Then toward the end of your career, and even into retirement, what matters is less the filthy lucre than doing what you believe in. We experience all three circles in different proportions at different times, and so getting a job might be more about choosing what's right for you at a certain period in your life than about defining you forever.

11

Falling in Love

When the eponymous and married heroine in Tolstoy's epic *Anna Karenina* falls for the dashing soldier Vronsky, there's a terrible irony. Only a short while before, Anna had been called in by her sister-in-law, Dolly, to save the marriage between Dolly and her husband, Anna's brother, threatened by his having an affair with the maid. The adultery doctor, Anna, herself becomes an adulteress, infected with the disease she had been called on to cure.

The irony lends itself to being read in a number of ways. Psychologically Anna is suggestible: for all the superficial virtue that prompts Dolly to get her involved, Anna has an underlying predisposition to infidelity. Something in her is susceptible to the idea of extramarital love, and when, thanks to her brother, she sees the idea embodied, it awakens in her a proclivity that might otherwise have lain dormant. That something is based on Anna's long-smothered yearning to escape from her own loveless marriage to a bureaucrat of striking *sang-froid*. Apprehending a super-abundance of romantic warmth in her brother's philandering, she wants a share to make up for her own lack of it. In this transition from seeming blandly good at the opening of the novel to becoming morally ambiguous, Anna acquires a psychological depth that, to use the handy classification of the English novelist and critic E. M. Forster, turns her into a character who is less "flat" and more "round."

Then there's an interpretation to do less with the motivations of its personae than with the structure of the book, a reading that's "typological." Her brother's indiscretion breaks the ground for Anna's: he is the *type* and she the *antitype*, in a pattern not dissimilar to that in *Romeo and Juliet* where Romeo has first to fall for the fantasy figure of Rosaline before succumbing to the real thing in Ms. Capulet. In such cases, a tacit acknowledgment of nothing less than the Christian Bible is at work, *typology* in this context referring to the relationship between an Old and a New Testament figure, like Adam and Christ, where the former represents a foreshadowing of the latter, who overshadows all. A lesser event prepares the way for a greater, like a warm-up act or a rehearsal. Thus Dolly's lighter problem paves the way for Anna's graver situation.

In case that seems like a purely technical point, typology, as well as shaping the book, is a device with which Tolstoy communicates an insight about love's nature: namely, that love runs a scale from domestic to dramatic. Where Dolly's dolors have a comic air, Anna's entanglement with Vronsky is pure tragedy, and because it's Anna who commands center stage, we are meant to deduce that when it comes to love, the more tragic, the truer. Anything less doesn't count as much, which means that with the purest love comes pain. Not unlike a religious calling, true love opens out into a higher dimension—a realm of rapture—but at the cost of self-sacrifice, vividly illustrated when Anna ends up throwing herself under a train.

Anna and her world might be fictional, but this love scale applies to their real-life counterparts, especially those falling in love for the first time, who might well wonder if what they're experiencing is the genuine article. The uncertainty is compounded by the fact that love is so peculiarly subjective that objective measures are hard to come by. Whereas we know from the fact of paracetamol's curing it that a headache, say, feels pretty much the same to everyone, love has nothing by which it can be scientifically tested. Is this love that I'm feeling, or an impersonator? Each love might conceivably be unique. Even if it does feel real, the emotion can be dismissed by elders as puppy love, and again because there's no proof, only personal protestation, such reactions can leave a poison sac of doubt in the lover's mind.

Part of the problem is that love lends itself happily to imitation, and that's because it displays easily observable symptoms: talking obsessively about the new person, listening to mushy music, staring off into space, writing poetry, and so on. Things that look like love might indeed be lookalikes, *faux-amis*, or frauds; which means that without much skill, one can affect being in love, and where that sac of doubt won't dissolve, it can be obscured by a bit of love acting. Just as a wedding with all the trimmings is supposedly more romantic, one can supplement love with these readily available gestures, and thus convince both the skeptics and the self of its validity. Besides, that scale of love, which privileges the extraordinary above the ordinary, creates a pressure for overstatement. One can't claim to be in love and, when interrogated, report that it's just "fine": it has to be amazing. In love, there's little place for doubt, or at least for the admitting of it.

Despite such potential for doubt, delusion, and drama, falling in love is arguably the most momentous event in one's life. For Anna Karenina, that's largely because she was already betrothed, and the admixture of new love with old marriage proved highly flammable. But the flames of love don't always need such complex kindling: a simple boy-meets-girl scenario can be enough. Either way, the event of falling in love releases a tsunami into an otherwise every-day picture, and of course, it can lead to more tangibly life-determining events like having children. It's one of the few things that can ultimately shape one's life as much as the conditions at its start—one's nationality, one's family, one's country of residence: in fact it has the power to redefine all three. When one falls in love, one's very destiny is at stake.

No wonder love unleashes a slew of feelings: delight, anxiety, anticipation, self-doubt, and so on. But it would be a mistake to think that love is defined by them. After all, we feel those things in different proportions on a more or less daily basis in relation to all sorts of unremarkable situations: getting the furnace fixed, chatting to one's young nephew, waiting for the results of a test. So what's different about love? It's the fact that such feelings get centered on another being. All one's otherwise divergent emotions suddenly converge on a single presence. Where, before falling in love, one's attentions were spread, albeit unevenly here and there, now a preeminent figure outstrips all others, as if from among the crowd a hitherto unacknowledged prince or princess steps forth. There's no love without a connection to a specific person, nor without a reckoning that esteems that person as most high. If it is an emotion, perhaps it's a variety of relief—relief that at last a personage has come forward to host all one's quivering hopes.

This ascribing inordinate value to another human being—what Freud wrote down as an "overestimation of the object"—is what ordinarily we refer to as *idealizing* someone. To friends and family, your chosen lover might look all too average, even undesirable, but for now at least you'll be deaf to criticism, and in him or her you'll see little other than unassailable rightness. Just as well: without some denial of reality, idealization wouldn't be idealization. If love had to confine itself to empirical evidence, it wouldn't get off the ground. Perhaps it's what allows us to shift up from liking to loving: liking can be very nice, but it carries a little too much realism to lift off toward love. They say love is blind, as though it might be better for it to be clear-sighted, but too much clarity would risk ruining its chances. By suppressing the less in favor of the more flattering truths about another person, love facilitates bonding, which implies that bonding depends on a strategic degree of mutual delusion. Not to put too fine a point on it, it's what allows us to be loved as well as to love.

If this positions love as either a fragile hoax or a ruse to keep the human race reproducing, it doesn't mean deeper movements aren't in play. For love touches the soul, disturbs and rearranges it; love is otherworldly, as if it inhabited a foreign time zone or a far-flung part of the universe. This other world is where the soul resides, for the soul, assuming it exists, is what both predates and survives our biological lives, is what overbrims the physical body and enjoys an inherent link with eternal time. As such, the soul offers a natural ally to love, which likes nothing more than to imagine its own perpetuity. When people talk about finding their "soul mate," for example, it's as if an archaic union had been reactivated. Love harks back to some long-forgotten past, some remote state of union. Lovers will often describe the sense of having known one another before.

Alongside such atavism, love engages the soul in its forward look out into infinity, with lovers also talking compulsively about their love lasting forever. Joyous as it is, to say "I love you" therefore means acknowledging one's mortality, that there's something—love itself—that's capable of lasting beyond the end of life. Indeed there's an ancient tradition, stretching back to Plato and beyond, that construes love as a kind of ladder running up and down between humans and gods. As if standing on the ladder's lower rungs, lovers look up and get an intimation of the immortal and eternal sphere of the divine that might otherwise remain beyond reach. Which suggests that romantic love, rather than being merely human, sets us out on an ascent toward something even higher and perhaps infinite. It's not that human love, be it erotic or just friendly, is *different* from divine love; rather it's a route toward it. The idea gets taken forward in Christianity, where Jesus, whose role was to mediate between heaven and earth—to shuttle up and down the ladder—preaches a doctrine with love at its center. Directed even or especially toward one's enemies, the practice of love is the one most likely—more likely than being rich or famous, say—to win us everlasting life at the right hand of God. Some theologians go further, interpreting the whole world as an emanation of God's love. In a variation of the argument, the philosopher Benedict de Spinoza argued that God was present in everything around us, and that our being able to love this presence was the highest virtue we might achieve. In all cases, love on earth provides a foretaste of the heaven to come—itself a kind of typology. It is earthly, but it looks up.

Precisely because it is played out on the earth, this soul aspect of love will always be tethered to its worldly experience. Like a flower, love turns up toward the sun but remains rooted in the soil. Too much so, perhaps, for the earthly aspects of love, such as desire and longing, often cause suffering, hence those Karenina-like feelings of anxiety, and hence too the more general *bouleversement*, as the French say, the disorientation that comes with love. In a way, love never becomes soulful enough, never achieves the serenity glimpsed, because there's an earthly relationship to manage in the meantime. After a while one passes from being in love with someone to simply loving him or her, at which point things calm down again. But during the appropriately named fall into love, all is topsy-turvy.

One reason for this unsettling has little to do with the soul or the emotions at all. It's simply that falling in love, as a rite of passage, is designed to reorient where you belong, to realign your kinship grid, so to speak. This makes it different from most milestones apart from birth, which is the original setting-out. Traditionally falling in love marks the period of flux between living at home with your parents and settling down with a spouse, a kind of unruly interregnum when things are up in the air. If love has a function, it might be to effect an unfreezing in one's family system, before it refreezes again; bonds are broken as well as made, and the process can be disorienting. Even though most people today will fall in love several times before setting up house, every relationship still begins more or less as if it's the last, and so the rule of necessary upheaval continues to apply.

There's a worse *bouleversement*, however, that can be more literally tragic. It happens when the love is unrequited and the suffering contains little sweetness of any kind. Its most celebrated portrayal comes in Goethe's *Sor-*

rows of Young Werther. The young protagonist simply cannot influence his beloved Charlotte to look on him as anything more than a charming friend, and while he is waiting for her, she proceeds to marry his rival. Werther takes a pistol and with it brings his short life to an end, simultaneously triggering a fashion for romantic suicides among Goethe's real-world readership. The message is that feelings of love, especially where unrequited, can be too much for one person, and this takes us back to the question of how to demonstrate that love exists. If love is so easily imitable, how does a suitor persuade his beloved of the sincerity of his feelings? Suicide at least proves the love authentic, even as it preempts for good the possibility of its being returned.

Clearly, the waiting for love can be ruinous, and for Roland Barthes, the French author of *A Lover's Discourse*, which refers a great deal to Goethe's cautionary tale, waiting provides a key emblem of love—even when the love is requited. Because love is a kind of addiction, having to wait for one's fix can be intolerable. When you're in love, all you want is more; life spent apart from the beloved barely counts as life at all. Barthes describes it as a "tumult of anxiety provoked by waiting for the loved being, subject to trivial delays (rendezvous, letters, telephone calls, returns)." Like the experience of the child who stares longingly at the chocolate cake but first has to eat her greens, this having to wait feels less like the moderate deferral of an indulgent pleasure than being deprived of a vital right that makes life worth living. A tumult it is, and young lovers mark their time not according to the clock but the time spent with or without the precious one; everything becomes about how much time together they have left and when they will next see each other. The beloved becomes the reference point for all activity, making the clock go slowly when you're not together and race around the dial when you are.

With regard to waiting, Barthes quotes an imaginary lover saying to himself, "Am I in love?—Yes, since I am waiting." This is Barthes's larger and more innovative point. Rather than starting with the feelings of love and then finding ways to express it, Barthes suggests that lovers operate from the other end of the telescope. You're in love with someone because you're waiting for her, not because she's actually your ideal: this is the opposite of waiting for someone because you're in love. The outward behavior drives the inner condition. In fact the whole trajectory of love is guided more by these stock behaviors than by personal motives, which explains why love goes through such predictable phases. We might think love is all about free feeling and spontaneous expression, but it has a program of its own that more or less every relationship then enacts. In other words, Barthes sees love as a series of stereotypical feints that we have to perform for the love to count as love. Again this raises the issue of fakery, for there's that confusion of real love with its theatrical equivalents. Having said that, Barthes's point is more subtle: love is *both* real *and* pastiche. Its melodrama is part of its essence, and there's no love that doesn't act itself out as such.

Among the standard actions adopted by lovers perhaps the most pivotal is declaring "I love you." It is the linguistic apex, the statement that no other statement in love can trump. You could even argue that until the three magic words are spoken, the lovers aren't actually in love. After all, if you can't tell your lover that you love him, can you really claim the love is real? You might feel love in your heart, but because love has this performative character, you need to come out and say it. The loving is in the saying. In the case of first love, declaring one's love is almost tantamount to losing one's virginity, and possibly more precious. Yes, virginity is the rarer resource in that it can be traded only once, as it were, whereas the phrase "I love you" can be repeated without becoming significantly devalued—with the proviso that declarations of love to former lovers have to count for less than declarations to the incumbent. Nevertheless because a declaration of love involves the soul as much as the body, the stakes become that much higher. Technically "I love you" might be as hackneyed as any other phrase in the language, yet because of what it means it's always spoken as though it might never be repeated, as though each enunciation might be unique. The phrase needs to sound as unprecedented and as unrepeatably special as the love itself.

What's so odd today is that this sense of the unique experience of love coincides with the common knowledge that love can indeed befall you more than once in a lifetime. In this sense *Anna Karenina* heralds the modern age, and "first love" is precisely that: first but not last. As people live longer, become more affluent, and are aware of increased choice, there's a much more developed sense of love being a pleasure to be refreshed periodically, like buying a new house. And yet first love is special, an exercise of the soul that both recalls the munificence and warmth of being a child and introduces the sense of oneself as a grown-up, as someone who might make a journey through life with someone you didn't start life with. You become yourself with another self: you make a pair, and in doing so you see the future in each other's eyes.

12

Tying the Knot

There's an episode of the American comedy *Curb Your Enthusiasm* in which Larry David, who plays himself, renews his wedding vows. It's his wife's idea, and it takes Larry a while to warm to it, but in the end he agrees, only to find the ceremony requires him to pledge his love "for all eternity." Being Larry, he can't let that pass. At the original wedding service, ten years earlier, he had agreed to wed merely "until death do us part." Clearly, between death and eternity lies an infinite gap. Perhaps he's thinking eternity might be a good place to meet someone else.

Though comic, the situation raises questions about marriage that aren't entirely unserious. Why is death and not eternity the usual term for the marriage contract? Presumably it's because after death, if you belong to anyone, you belong to God or at least the universe. Besides, it's odd to imagine heaven full of married couples, a heaven that for many might be hell. Could the individuals behave in heavenly fashion if shackled to their other half, ready to call them on their faults and almost literally drag them down to earth? Probably not. By implication, marriage has a worldly character, constitutes a pragmatic structure for the raising of children and the keeping of sex within respectable limits. From a human perspective, it might seem terribly romantic, all-encompassing, or sublime, but seen from loftier heights, marriage is but the convenient pair-bonding that offers the least bad social arrangement for time spent on earth.

So Larry David might be right to be skeptical, if on grounds other than he'd cite. Sweet as his wife's sentiments about eternal love might be, they don't stack up: marriage is for life, and only life. Indeed recognizing that with death the relationship must end gives marriage much of its human pathos. The vows say "I'll love you for as long as I possibly can. I can't love you after I'm dead, because I'll be dead." Marriage begins from death, as it were, and works backward to fill the intervening period with love. Were there no limit on that love—were marriage actually to be eternal—it would lose the requisite tension for commitment. After all, you needn't commit to somebody if you're never going to lose each other; it's redundant.

So Larry goes ahead with the service and makes his vow, just as he had at his wedding. Which raises the second question: What was so deficient about the first promise that it had to be renewed and extended? Do promises go stale? Surely the whole point of a promise is that, as long as it's not broken, it remains fresh—fresh as on the day it was made. That's what a promise is, in part, a way of resisting time, of withstanding the changes in circumstances that threaten to undo the good intent the promise had inscribed. It's in the face of caprice that a promise is made, declaring that it will be fulfilled come what may. By referring equally to scenarios of sickness and health, of wealth and poverty, the marriage service spells it out: it asks bride and groom to agree that in the midst of change, each will remain constant.

This steadfast quality of the promise has stimulated several philosophers to ruminate upon it. First perhaps was St.

Augustine, who wrote about the promise one makes to be faithful to God. Compared with this higher devotion— nuns speak of being married to the Church or to Jesus or to God himself—getting married is indeed the more worldly option, yet appears modeled on it. The noble fidelity to your spouse echoes the commitment to God, and in this sense the promise at marriage is divine. It shows you've got the moral fiber to think beyond the temptations that way- lay others and stick to the one true path of attachment to your mate. This makes promising a direct expression of vir- tue; indeed the word *vice*, the opposite of virtue, literally means a "turning," as if allowing one's head to be turned or seduced by siren songs along the way. Promising, like virtue, is about straightness and strength, about not deviating from the sworn-to direction. In the most everyday setting, the person who says "I promise" can expect moral approbation.

But promising also enjoys less virtuous aspects which nevertheless do not detract from its power. For Friedrich Nietzsche—a thinker almost diametrically opposed to Augustine—to make a promise was to resist all dogma about "virtue," along with any religious connotations. When we promise, we declare an intent to master the future with our will, to subdue the future vicissitudes of life to a personal vision of what that life should look like. Rather than falling in with whatever the future might hold or kowtowing to some abstract notion of a good life to emulate, we do some- thing active: we announce that we will make an aspiration come true, that we will control future eventualities that might otherwise control us or toss us about on an ocean of fate or someone else's agenda. Promising and willing are in this respect identical, and of course the phrase "I will" features prominently in versions of the marriage service. In promising, the future, otherwise so wide and ungraspable, gets appropriated and tamed; for Nietzsche this meant that it's also taken away from anyone else, particularly an institution like the Church, which might claim some authority over that future. By getting married, bride and groom agree to own their own fate as husband and wife, without external help. Observing this moment of empowerment, Nietzsche might prefer it was an individual rather than a couple swearing the oath, but the logic carries over. Promising demonstrates strength of character, an unafraid energy for bending the world according to one's will.

Much influenced by Nietzsche, several twentieth-century thinkers took up their predecessor's ideas but tried to stitch back in the moral backbone that Nietzsche had been so keen to excise. Yes, a promise (including a marriage promise) throws a net over the future, so to speak, gives it a shape and draws it tight, but just as important it throws a net over another person. If marriage is about committing to the *future* together, it's as much about committing to the future *together*. A promise doesn't happen in isolation: we only ever promise in relation to an other, even if that other is ourself. A New Year's resolution, for example, is a promise to oneself, whereby we divide the self in half, so that one of us acts while the other one of us holds the first one to account. Without this relation to another there would be no accountability, and a promise without accountability is not a promise, but idle reverie. To take a more ordinary example, if I promise to pay back the money I owe you, I am now in a relationship with you, in the sense that between us an active tension now applies—not an emotional tension, but the built-in tension of having business that hasn't been settled. This unsettled tension is a good thing, because it generates authentic contact between people; debtor or creditor, both have an interest in each other. What's more, the promise asks each to do right by the other—in this case, for me to pay back the money on time and for you not to charge interest at an extortionate rate. Hence the promise's moral quality, a quality that in marriage only redoubles, because the vows typically require bride and groom to commit not just money ("worldly goods") to each other, but body and soul. Marriage constitutes a kind of absolute debt flowing two ways, and because both parties are indebted, both are, in principle at least, more likely to act well.

To test it, one could flip the argument over and ask what would happen if we never made promises, of the marrying kind or not. For in a sense all relationships have promises as their foundation, even if they are unwritten: that I'll be nice to you when I see you, that I'll see you not fewer than x times within a period of y, and so on. It's how our expectations get formed. What's unique about marriage is precisely that it does make the promise written—and of course spoken. The marriage promise is public, and the holding to account extends to the wider community. Even when the marriage takes place in private and with the minimal paraphernalia—bride, groom, official, and witness—it's still technically public, a bridal broadcast. That's partly to root out any bigamy or similarly felonious skeleton, but it's also because in being witnessed the newlyweds will feel all the more responsible for making the marriage work. One can't get married in the metaphorical dark, and those couples who elope to escape the eyes of their family will still find that, to be legitimate, the marriage requires a witness. Besides, promises are made morally if not legally stronger when others are involved, if only because breaking them will have an impact on the witnesses too, who in their own way will have become invested in the union.

Thus the marriage promise binds bride and groom on three radials: to the future, to each other, and to the witnesses. And if a wedding has necessarily to be witnessed, small wonder it becomes so intensely visual an event. What starts as a legal requirement swiftly escalates into a piece of theater, the wedding recorded by everything from the mind's eye of each guest, to the official photographer, to the mobile phone camera in each of those guests' pockets. Apart from the birth of a baby, and perhaps a graduation, there are few milestones we document so zealously as the ceremony of marriage—much more than passing your driving test, say, or getting a job. Perhaps that's because it's so fundamentally shareable as an occasion, with so many people feeling part of it. An unrecorded wedding is practically unthinkable, with the consequence that self-consciousness besets the wedding party, who respond by dressing up for the occasion. And now that they're dressed up, the witnesses/guests want all the more to gawk at them, and themselves dress up more in response, thus becoming more visually compelling to the other guests, who then all gawk at each other. The optical feast whets the appetite it slakes, and the main activity at a wedding becomes not eating or dancing, but looking.

Preeminent in this exponential scopophilia, this festival of looks, is the figure of the bride, she who reigns as icon for the day, with all the adulation, adoration, and attention that implies. All sight lines gather in on her, the gently sashaying focus of every pair of eyes. Does this explain what in Western cultures is the traditional whiteness of her costume? Sure, the bridal gown symbolizes purity, but given the intensity of regard that the bride gladly suffers, perhaps only white is sufficiently neutral not to color, literally, the fantasies directed onto her quasi-regal being. Strangely, it makes her as generic as she is special. On the one hand, she's the most exposed, viewed, exhibited, photographed, remarked-upon personage at the event; on the other hand, the radiant whiteness causes her almost to disappear and become identified just as "the bride" rather than by her own name.

This play of appearance and disappearance, of presence and absence, converges especially in the veil she so delicately wears over her face. In alluding to the tensile guard of the hymen, the veil too evokes virginity, and with it the tension between the bride being and not being given to her husband. It's significant, therefore, that the veil never fully obscures the face. Whether translucent or opaque but leaving the eyes visible, the veil communicates that the bride is in equal measures available and unavailable. In this the veil enjoys a close link with the words *nuptial* and *nubile*, which both have been argued to refer to clouds, that is, a not entirely impenetrable covering of the sky. During the vows the veil should remain solemnly in place, merely hinting at its uncovering; only when the rite has been cemented with the exchange of rings can the veil be lifted for the kiss that confirms the transition from ambiguous withdrawal to full presence—and that plays its own part in prefiguring the more intimate consummation to come.

Of course, the notion of the bride being "given" to the groom has been attacked for its chauvinism, and a vast body of anthropological literature has analyzed the gifts, human or otherwise, given in marriage. Like it or not, marriage involves an economic as well as a romantic settlement, involving the sharing and division of capital, and with it the opportunity for the parties involved to augment their wealth. In this sense a wedding, as the inauguration of marriage, provides an opportunity to allude to each family's net worth, something of which the guests will be acutely aware as they reckon up the cost of the flowers, marquee, and champagne. These days that marriage capital will more likely take the form of equity held by each partner in a property than a casket of silver, but it's the same notion of an implicit asset base to fund the new enterprise that is a husband-and-wife partnership.

Do these economic considerations undermine the romance? We are inclined to say yes, but one has only to go back to the time of Jane Austen, say, to appreciate how tightly interwoven the two have long been. In chapter after chapter the reader follows the painstaking analysis of the financial advantages and disadvantages of marriage, and how these factors, in conjunction with the romantic sentiments involved, produce such a very fine algorithm for determining whether or not to marry a person. Love and money formed part of a single calculation, heart and head whirring in a rapid oscillation that blurred the distinction between them. Not that the separation of the two hadn't already been envisaged. Austen's compatriot William Hogarth painted pictures half a century before her, warning of the dire consequences of marriage made purely for money. Peopled by corpulent capitalists, avaricious attorneys, and syphilitic sybarites, they make it clear that money is a poisonous worm that burrows into the heart and fatally infects it.

By contrast, when a marriage is made out of pure love, naïve or implausible as it may sound to skeptical ears, that love gets not only confirmed but transfigured. Of course, intense love can be found outside marriage—and for many it's marriage that corrupts love—yet even the most secular, anti-authoritarian lovers will still seek out forms of ceremony to solemnize their feelings for one another. This "ceremony" need only consist in saying "I love you": the point is that deeply felt romantic love, no matter how febrile, appears to yearn for the momentary stillness, formality, and gravitas that comes with the love being stated as such. Even something as otherwise superficial as the Las Vegas wedding has its few seconds of seriousness; the surface needs this depth, albeit brief, to underwrite it. This stating affords love the permanence it fears it may never achieve; the triumph of marriage is to make this permanence real, to preserve the otherwise too fluid and transient feelings that love incites. And this defines a happy marriage: the continuance of love over time.

Hence perhaps the affinity of love with poetry, that form of language that most aspires to permanence—and hence too why poems often get read at weddings. For the most profound wedding poem of all, nothing has yet to exceed the ancient *Song of Songs*. Written either by or for King Solomon, this epithalamium (the technical term for a wedding song) forms one of the books of the Hebrew Bible, although its lack of explicitly religious content has led commentators to question its inclusion. The song's defenders argue that the sensuous, even erotic exchange between bride and groom, which makes up the majority of the poem, forms an allegory of the love between God and humanity, or God and the Church. Be that as it may, the poem stands on its own literary merit, and it sheds light on the meaning of marriage.

Not least striking is that the song emphasizes the bride's admiring of the groom as much as his of her, thus redressing the modern obsession with the woman in white at the expense of the often overlooked husband-to-be. As such, it brings harmony and balance. The bride says:

My beloved is white and ruddy,
the chiefest among ten thousands.
His head is as the most fine gold;
his locks are bushy, and black as a raven:
his eyes are as the eyes of doves by the rivers of waters,
washed with milk, and fitly set:
his cheeks are as a bed of spices, as sweet flowers;
his lips like lilies, dropping sweet-smelling myrrh:
his hands are as gold rings set with beryl;
his belly is as bright ivory overlaid with sapphire:
his legs are as pillars of marble, set upon sockets of fine
       gold:
his countenance is as Lebanon, excellent as the cedars:
his mouth is most sweet:
yea, he is altogether lovely.

Because the verse makes space for the bride to express her erotic feelings, it also counts as thoroughly modern. Her passion breathes through the lines, thus casting her virginity as a state of barely restrained sexual intent rather than chaste demurral. We talk about "tying the knot" as a metaphor for making a commitment, but it's not explicit in the metaphor that the commitment is as physical as it is emotional or practical. Here that commitment is underpinned by a compelling sensuousness whereby marriage, rather than leading to the gradual thinning-out of love, concentrates its already heady power. By glossing over this erotic aspect of marriage, modern weddings tend to occlude the very thing that got the couple to want to knot together in the first place.

In fact the lines go beyond love: it's total adoration. The bride may as well be praising a god, just as the groom had lauded her as if she were a goddess. Each spouse becomes an icon for the other, and the imagery of jewels, of glittering stones that endure through time, points again to a permanence that the marriage contract, as opposed to a mere "relationship," then does its best to capture. It's as if marriage were a domestic religion, in which each spouse worships the other in imitation of the more properly divine. There's something about being wife and husband—as opposed to girlfriend and boyfriend—that carries a comparative grandeur, a grandeur to do with marriage's defining intent to endure. Something as ordinary as marriage embodies the extraordinary.

This brings us back full circle to the notion of being married for eternity. It's an illusion, of course, and Larry David was right to be skeptical. Tragically, it needs only one of the partners to die for the marriage, at the very same stroke, to end. It may take a while to adjust to the fact, but for all his or her devotion to the dead spouse, the widower or widow is no longer married from that very instant. In this sense marriage is just a breakable shell mounted around the inevitable fate of each human in his or her fundamental isolation and mortality. On the other hand, marriage behaves as if it were eternal, and it creates a sense of shared destiny that might just carry on, despite the obvious and empirical boundary placed on it by the death of its two participants. When we marry, we touch on the not shameful but noble deceit that we will outlive ourselves, and that we'll stay with the person we love forever.

13

Having Children

The U.S. Census Bureau regularly publishes its forecast of world population figures. Here were the first seven months of 2010 (month/day/year):

> 01/01/10: 6,793,593,686
> 02/01/10: 6,799,929,555
> 03/01/10: 6,805,652,275
> 04/01/10: 6,811,988,144
> 05/01/10: 6,818,119,630
> 06/01/10: 6,824,455,499
> 07/01/10: 6,830,586,985

Being population figures, they take into account both births and deaths: every month the world accumulates another 6 million people, or about 200,000 per day, 8,000 or so per hour, 140 per minute, or just over two per second. Of course, with infinite resources, so staggering a rate of reproduction wouldn't matter, but environmental warnings about the dwindling of such resources abound. Less apparent is what's driving the urge to have children on such a colossal scale.

To be fair, it's not the world as a whole that says "We want more children"; it's individuals deciding from a parochial rather than a global perspective to have kids, with the aggregate of all those small decisions adding up to a big crisis. The crisis might sound peculiarly modern, but this catastrophic de-link between personal and public responsibility picks up on the *categorical imperative* as advanced by the German philosopher Immanuel Kant (whom we last saw discussing the sublime) over two hundred years ago. That doctrine says you should only do things that you'd want everybody else to do as well. Act as though each action were to become a law, or an *imperative*, by which others shall be bound. So have children if you like, but doing so implies that you'd like everyone else to be required to do the same. In folk terms, the message is "Lead by example."

That's hard to disagree with, but typically we act according not to the categorical but to its poor relation, what Kant called the *hypothetical imperative*, which conveniently forgets that our individual actions should be a model for everyone. In this mode, we see the world as a means of achieving our own ends, that is, having children regardless; in particular we fail to register that other people, no matter how far-flung, have rights and desires as legitimate as our own. With a few exceptions that include China during the period when it imposed on its own burgeoning populace a one-child rule, no official law of birth control was ever enforced to make the categorical imperative—of restraining your reproductive reflex—imperative. Certain countries (and religions) even encourage people to manufacture little ones, though such drivers are external. And so we collapse back to the personal and the parochial, influenced more by our immediate peers than global brethren, making decisions to increase our family even if doing so might lead to wars over resources between the children that ensue.

So, from within this shorter horizon of personal interest, whence the desire to have children? The evolutionary answer for reproduction might be furthering the species, but this also fails the Kantian test of leading by example: you wouldn't want everyone to be furthering the species at the same time because that very species would run out of those dwindling resources pretty quickly. And yet it's not difficult to concede that wanting children might involve an *instinct*, whereby you're hypnotized by the species into yearning to procreate. Then there's the brute fact that the route to having children passes through sex, and there are almost certainly instincts, or at least cravings, for that. But the appetite for sex isn't at all the same as the aspiration to have children; the libido serves a more urgent and impetuous master than the far-sighted figure who presents us with a vision of our own family-to-be.

Over and above evolutionary and libidinal motives, therefore, there may well be an intrinsically sentimental element in the desire to have children, even if it's accompanied by economic considerations ranging from "How can we afford to keep them?" to "How long before we can we get them working for us?" In this sentimental mode, the mind, like a house, fills with the patter of tiny feet, the sound of children laughing, the daily delights of family life. No doubt part of such sentiment can also be explained in evolutionary terms—as the emotional associate of that sexual agent working on the species' behalf—but other parts may be unique. Namely, that having an idealized picture of the future might be a prerequisite for acting in favor of it, and if the desire to have children depends on seeing them first in the mind's eye, so be it. Children exist in the imagination before they exist in reality. In fact they are the future itself—there is no future without children—and so a picture of one's offspring-to-be holds more power than, say, the vision of the house you want to buy. To be sentimental about having children is to love the future as embodied by them.

Not to mention the love of the children themselves. Kant's fellow German philosopher, G. W. F. Hegel, believed these sentiments about family life to be crucial. The love for one's children, and the love within a family, works on a quite different scale from other kinds of love—it is not tempestuous or "romantic." But precisely because it grounds love in the domestic, it makes it more real and valuable. As it happens, Hegel did believe that larger forces, analogous to evolution, were at work, whereby the love within a family was propelled by a greater spirit in the world, a spirit with a need to implant itself in real people and so mitigate its own otherwise abstract nature. A spirit that remains a spirit isn't much good to anybody: it needs to give spirit to something. Not unlike saying the species manipulates the individual into having children, Hegel thought the *world spirit* had to realize itself as love, and that the family might best keep that spirit going by turning the love between husband and wife into living children.

Specifically Hegel says, "It is only in the children that the unity [of the marriage] exists externally, objectively, and explicitly as a unity, because they love the children as their love, as the embodiment of their own substance." Childless couples might protest, but Hegel is arguing that until a man-woman partnership produces offspring, their love for each other hasn't realized itself. The child stands as a mirror to the relationship between its parents, reflecting back a completeness between Mom and Dad that on their own they wouldn't be able to behold. What's more, they "love the children as their love": their own love now opens a channel to and from their child, and a circuit of loving forms, in which the love between parents can't be separated from their love of the child. The child completes the parents, and so, in this sense, the motive for having children is to supplement the gap in love that exists in marriage. Not having children, in the Hegelian view, implies a lacuna in the very quality of the love enjoyed by a couple. Having them means that love, which is the character of the world spirit, realizes itself through the family, and the family completes the couple.

Profound as his theory sounds, what Hegel stresses less is a motive for having kids that's perhaps even deeper. By definition, children come after their parents and are younger, which means they are likely to outlive them. Tragically, there's no guarantee the parents won't survive their children, but in terms of motive, one expects on becoming a parent to inaugurate a human life that will continue after one's own passing away. This opens up two kinds of future. The first is that of the child in its own right; the second is that of the parents as carried forward in both the genes and the memory of their surviving child. These provide immense gratification. In the first, the parents launch their child forward, so to speak, hoping the best for it, while watching from behind. They urge it on to make the most of life and of its life. In fact this urge on the part of parents is almost an urge for life itself, for life to continue as represented in their child. The feeling that there is more life to come makes the parents better able to bear their own death, which now becomes a necessary falling-away to make space for the life that continues after them. They are separate from the child and detachable, like the part of the space shuttle that gets jettisoned, allowing the main engine to power onward. The future in this scenario belongs to the child at the deliberate and willing expense and exclusion of its parents, whose role is mainly to bless that future.

The second future doesn't exclude but rather includes the parents in the life of the surviving child. Because children are made from their parents, are nothing but the physical combination of their mother and father, they necessarily bear their parents within them, and continue to do so long after the parents pass away. Today we refer to this afterlife of the parents as the *genetic inheritance* of the child, but such scientific language can obscure the more basic and astonishing fact that the parents actually live on through their children, just as the parents represented the living-on of their own parents previously. This implies, bizarrely enough, that generations don't just succeed one another; they coexist in the present. To be alive means to host one's ancestors in one's physical being. Having children thus prolongs an organic chain and secures a certain kind of immortality for the parents. This isn't the same as *legacy*: it's not about objects or achievements that can be pointed to and that outlast their makers; it's about an internal extension of the life of the parent within the child. Nor does this count as parental vanity, the desire to see one's own image repeated down the generations, as if an inexhaustible biological photocopier could be pressed into the parents' service. It's more primal: a longing for the quick of life, the animating spirit of the parent, never to be quenched, even after the parent's own inevitable demise. And again, as in Hegel, that spirit has to take bodily form.

There's a third future too. For whether children remember their parents thus becomes secondary; they *are* the memory, which means their hosting of the lives of their parents is not just physical. A child is the memory of its parents, and so essential is this fact that the parents themselves don't need to die for it to be true. From its date of birth, the child is the memory, the recombined archive, of those who created it. Because of this, we could add to Hegel's formula about the child completing the love between the parents; we could also say that children reflect back to their parents not just their love, but the fact that their parents will be survived. In their children parents see a memory of themselves, as if their death had already taken place.

Of course, what gets passed on isn't just genes. Having children also means encumbering one's offspring with a goodly number of one's character defects. As Philip Larkin so pithily put it:

> *They fuck you up, your mum and dad.*
> *They may not mean to, but they do.*

A child may or may not constitute a clean slate, but whether smooth or already marked, that slate cannot but accrue psychological graffiti, courtesy of its parents, from the early years onward. Hence a delicate balancing act is often required of those parents, caught between trying not to pass on their own flaws and seeking to inculcate in their children the set of values they have developed. To have a child is to make a fresh moral and psychological start. In this sense every child is expected to redeem its parents, or at least give them the chance to do things differently and thus correct the errors of the benighted grandparents in the previous generation who fucked the parents up in the first place.

Not that it's all progress. This weight of redemption can become oppressive. Children don't exist to save their parents, even if, as in Hegel, they might complete their love, and developmental psychology abounds in literature that cautions parents against exploiting their children to assuage their own neediness. A needy parent restricts the emotional growth of the child by crowding out its inchoate concerns, demanding attention and thus distracting the child from its own undisturbed development. In the terms of the British psychoanalyst John Bowlby, the *attachment* made between parent and child becomes insecure, because too much anxiety gets in the way. Bowlby doesn't put it like this, but it's right that a child should be "selfish," because otherwise the self would not develop; when the parent is the selfish one, the child is forced to abandon its own unconscious project of emotional growth, not to mention the inappropriate reversal of roles. So if the parents are fucked up, the onus rests with them to work it out in private, not employ the kid as a means of attenuating their issues.

Such concepts are taken up and extended in other branches of psychoanalysis, which has its own theories about sparing children from parental craziness. In brief, the parent acts the superego, the psychic policeman to the child's ego: the parent regulates the child's wishes, and in so doing shows the child what does and doesn't constitute socially acceptable behavior. It's this taming of the wild child by the parent that creates the good society, a commons of grown-ups who've learned *not* to be constantly selfish, as it happens. However, when the regulation tips over and becomes too severe, the parents don't just suppress and channel the child's otherwise reckless and selfish ambitions, they force the child into repressing its desires altogether. These repressed desires then build up and from time to time explode, thus impairing, not improving, the child's social performance. Accordingly parents shouldn't just say "Don't do that," they should also say "Do this instead," and thus help the child find alternative outlets for its energies. From this perspective, having children positions the parents as guardians not just of their children but of the society those children are set to join; their main role is to normalize any aberrance on the part of their progeny and so produce citizens whose behavior conforms to that which prevails.

There's even a version of psychoanalysis that connects this notion of repressed desire in children to the question of what's passed down between the generations. I'm referring to the extraordinary work of Nicolas Abraham and Maria Torok, Hungarian analysts of the later twentieth century. They argue that what gets passed on is nothing less than the repressed material itself, creating a phenomenon known as *transgenerational haunting*. When the parents were children they were dealt with too severely by their own parents, and so repressed their wishes. These wishes went to form the unconscious, but instead of erupting every now and then in outbursts of bad behavior, they remain repressed and get passed on, like secrets, to their own children—children who never become aware of the secrets as such, but even so give off a sense of being haunted by the previous generation. Such secrets can take various forms, but we all carry them to a greater or lesser extent. To illustrate the point, Abraham and Torok invoke Shakespeare's *Hamlet*, arguing that what causes the prince's sociopathic behavior is a secret he has inherited from his father, the ghost, that he cannot quite apprehend. If in Shakespeare's tragedy Prince Hamlet is first and foremost a son (the play is called *Hamlet, Prince of Denmark*), what's tragic is that the son takes on the sins of the father, as it were, without ever knowing he has done so or what the sin is. The prince mistakenly apportions the wrongdoing to his mother and stepfather; he's got as far as smelling a rat, but believes it to be located somewhere other than where it actually is. It's his father who was the guilty thing, with the child Hamlet unwittingly forced to carry that guilt within him. If the prince is haunted, it's by this enigmatic secret held by his father, not by himself. All the more reason, therefore, to ensure that when you do have children, you're as little fucked up as possible: your very secrets could get passed down the line without ever being decrypted.

Beneath all such considerations runs the issue of whether children merely repeat or substantially improve on the life of their parents, a question that in turn taps into the historical conundrum as to whether the world is fundamentally getting better or is doomed to recycle or even reverse history. It's unverifiable, of course, and psychologically it leads to another finely balanced question for parents: to what extent they want their children effectively to be the same as themselves or not. Yes, a parent wishes the best for the child, wishes at a minimum for the child's quality of life to equal his or her own, but does hoping your child has a better life include allowing it to be quite a different person? The art of parenting no doubt involves a subtle trade-off between holding on and letting go, but what if the letting-go leads to having a child whom the parent considers alien? Don't all parents secretly hope to create somewhat improved versions of themselves? Happier, yes, but fundamentally the same?

If so, this means that despite that necessary link between them and the future, children always bring up the past—the ideal past, that is, the vision of a time of innocence, happiness, and plenty before everything got ruined. The wonderful future we want for our kids is nearly always a version of a past that never quite came about. It's as if, when a child is born, the mythological clock is turned back, and we could all start again. Despite the desire for the children to prosper and grow, parenting tends toward the conservative rather than progressive state of mind; for one's children one would always elect the contentment of peace over the challenges of innovation.

On the other hand, to have children is to have the future given back as unmade, as still replete with wondrous surprises, and on this note let me end the chapter with one of the most famous children's books of all time, *The Very Hungry Caterpillar*. It tells the story, as its title suggests, of a caterpillar who munches through several times its bodyweight in not just leaves and other organic matter, but also ice cream and cake. What makes the book so successful, among many other factors, is that it's not just *for* childhood, but *about* it. For once the caterpillar has consumed that vast menu of foodstuffs, and after a dreadful bellyache, it metamorphoses under the light of the moon into a "beautiful butterfly," with a double-page spread given over to the symmetrical wonder. The message to its child audience is that for all the confusion and strangeness you experience in the world of infancy, soon you shall outfly these sketchy beginnings and flourish. You too shall become a beautiful butterfly, a creature capable not only of independent flight but of a radiance that will be unique. And by the way, you should make sure you eat well.

The book carries equal doctrinal force for parents. It reminds them, first of all, that having children involves taking on some very hungry caterpillars, mouths to feed that are generally voracious. You as a parent will need to satisfy that insatiable appetite, without pause, and there's a not absurd risk that your children will eat you out of house and home. But the food also works as an allegory of sustenance that is emotional, with the book advising the parents to keep the kids supplied with all manner of ingredients, not just the serious stuff of fruit and veggies, but the frivolities, like that cake. Children require a balanced diet of the sane and the crazy, the practical and the imaginative, and it is up to the parents to provide it. The reward for this otherwise exorbitant need on the part of children to be fed with not just food but love and ideas is a final efflorescence in the shape of their own personal beauty.

Just as there is a miracle of birth, so, the book suggests, there is a miracle of development, whereby the pupa, the grub, the inert amoeba-like life-form that is the human baby, rapidly accelerates into an entity as enchanting as a mandala. What's particularly miraculous is that although the butterfly realizes the potential energy of the caterpillar, it connotes in turn a boundless sense of magic, its beauty working as a symbol of infinite exploration and joy. A natural phenomenon but also a work of art, the butterfly informs parents that having children means helping them become as extraordinary as they promised on the day their lives began.

14

Moving House

Did you hear about the man who, on learning that most accidents take place within the home, decided to move house?

Probably the worst accidents at home must be those involving fire, but they're not always such a bad thing. Rumi, the great thirteenth-century Sufi mystic, has a poem in which his house burning down makes him grateful. Why? It affords a better view of the rising moon. Apart from the pleasing aesthetic contrast in the poem between the lowliness of the earth and the loftiness of the night sky, there's an obvious message about the superiority of spiritual over earthly values, of holiness over housing.

What a long way we've come, or slipped, since Rumi. Today the word *house* has become synonymous with *property*, which suggests that rather than seeing it first and foremost as a home, we increasingly perceive our dwelling as a major object of ownership, something to stop burning down at all costs. Indeed the house has almost gotten elided with *capital*, for in some capitalist societies the house pretty directly represents equity or net worth, and this means that it hints in turn at how substantial we are as individuals. You have only to fill out an insurance form, with its rankings that place home owners above tenants, to appreciate the degree to which we equate the acquiring of property with the gaining of not just economic but social weight. Climbing the property ladder means ascending the societal rankings and, step by step, reinforcing one's general reputability.

Despite this trend upward, the way you then decorate your new pad will tend to remain pegged to the social class from which you hail. At least, this is the argument put forward by Pierre Bourdieu, the French sociologist, who argues that your choice of decor is an "opportunity to assert your position in social space." The iconic working-class example in Britain must be that of the three ceramic mallards nailed above the mantelpiece, placed equidistantly as if in flight. The intelligentsia might deride them as kitsch, but their owners see in them perhaps a soothing reference to English pastoral life, where such sentimentality itself is supposed to be a working-class trait. The ducks' equivalent among the minor aristocracy, say, might be the nineteenth-century watercolor of a fox hunt or the ancestral portrait, both designed to reflect the preeminent aristocratic value of heritage. To Bourdieu, such artifacts serve more to identify the class to which you belong than to encapsulate an objective aesthetic judgment.

Small wonder that moving house can cause such jumpiness. As you witness the moving van being loaded, more than chattel is being put onboard: that carpet bartered for in a Moroccan souk certainly holds sentimental value for you, but it also communicates your status as a confident urban traveler from the well-read bourgeoisie, the very kind of person who would scoff at mallards, or even appropriate them wittily to adorn the new loft apartment. And when the passerby watches you carefully tuck a Tizio lamp into a nook behind the Apple Mac computer, he or she will find the semiotics of your stuff confirmed. True, there's something about having all your belongings out on the pavement that makes them look arbitrary, as if a stage set is being taken apart at the end of a play, and yet each one of them says something about who you are. What's more, those very items will have seen you at your most authentic: crying in sorrow, falling asleep, taking that extra sweet, lying as you call in sick for work. Such objects don't just represent you, they know your secrets.

But there's a difference that, as it were, needs to be unpacked. It's between this portable paraphernalia—always more than you thought you had—and the house itself. Several languages make it obvious by classifying property as either movable or immovable. What you take with you might seem the less alienable precisely because it accompanies you wherever you are, but the immovable building will have literally housed your memories, and these don't easily dissolve. After all, it's chiefly at home that we bring up our children, entertain our friends, and have sex; even deaths and births may have taken place there. We leave these invisible prints upon the old house, and even after we've unloaded our movables into the new, the house continues to be strange because our history in it remains to be written.

Movable or not, *property* denotes the highly personal, and the etymology proves it. Most nearly captured in the French *propre*, which comes from Latin and indicates intimate possession, property is what's proper to one's very self. Conceivably this is because the sense of property emanates from a time before people moved so frequently, making a natural correspondence between where people lived and who they were. Just as surnames branded you a carter, wright, smith, or fletcher, so the house projected a facet of the self and provided a means of identification.

Such connections between the home and the self receive their most philosophical elaboration in an essay by Martin Heidegger, "Building Dwelling Thinking," a title deliberately without commas to suggest an isomorphic continuity among the three activities. It's worth saying that Heidegger's own dwelling place in the Black Forest, where he lived until his death in 1976, took on for him great significance. That his home was situated not far from where he was brought up, in Marburg, meant he was living out the precept he argued for, that people should remain close to their earthly origins. He argued this not out of knee-jerk conservatism—though he was deeply conservative—but because he isolated a necessary linkage between one's home on the earth and the very nature of Being (with a capital *B*). Where previous philosophers had, in Heidegger's view erroneously, abstracted out concepts like *being* and made them blandly universal or technical, he felt strongly that there is no Being that isn't rooted in time and place. And the place that matters most is the home, the dwelling, for it's in the dwelling that we naturally disclose what's most fundamental to us, which is our Being. The proverb "Home is where the heart is" thus takes on extra force, with the implication that exile from home means exile from what it is to be. Moving, especially if it means moving away from the place of one's childhood, might compromise something at the core.

More or less contemporary with Heidegger's thinking were the *Heimatfilme* or "homeland films" popular in 1950s Germany. Given the events of the prior decade, it's not surprising that the films celebrate a contented, rural neighborliness in retreat from the expansionist imperatives of wartime. Their scope is parochial, the sentiment one of consolation, and behind them all hums a subaudible drone of homeliness, as signaled by the word *Heimat*. They summon up a time, no doubt imaginary, when things were less complicated, when any sense that village life might be in thrall to political forces or that peasants are exploited is suppressed. *Home* thus signals an antitechnocratic space, an unadorned environment for cordial, unambitious relations within and between families who admit little difference or conflict among themselves.

I mentioned Heidegger's conservatism—for a period he even supported the Nazis—and in his theory of the home, which provides as it were the theoretical justification for the more instinctive celebration of *Heimat*, critics have detected less rational philosophy than a covert nostalgia no more evolved than in the films and, far worse, sinister racist undertones. As if he'd developed a highly sophisticated NIMBYism, Heidegger's insistence on staying close by the precincts of one's native soil barely disguises an ideal of ethnic purity and a mistrust of what's foreign. Superficially "native soil" might strike us as the most natural of notions, but it's highly historical: as people set up home in the territory where they were born, and their descendants follow suit, the place over time takes on the characteristics of its inhabitants, who then seek to defend the homeland as though it were a birthright. By the same token, moving house gets associated with both transience and transients, with a rootlessness to be feared or, worst-case scenario, vilified. About people who move a lot there's something discomfiting, and if insurance companies like home owners, then credit rating agencies just love people who stay put.

Against this conservatism there's an alternative tradition that takes a more skeptical view of home. Set aside the empirical point that Germany, like Britain, the United States, and so many other so-called homelands, hosts a people who, far from being indigenous or native, constitute the issue of centuries of miscegenation. For all but the most native of natives, an unalloyed, undivided "home" constitutes no more than a fantasy. Take instead the thinking of the French philosopher Emmanuel Levinas, somewhat junior to Heidegger, much influenced by him but also much unsettled. In simple terms, the nostalgic accent on the home, and on sameness, and on the concomitant suspicion of the outsider, flies in the face of what Levinas holds most dear, namely the need for us to welcome in the other. Because the home readily encourages on the part of its owner a defensive disposition ("Every man's home in his castle") and may tend as much to hostility as hospitality, it's quite likely to rebuff the other, so it is better for us, ethically speaking, if we wean ourselves off the otherwise compelling vision of a homeland. In this sense, moving house should never be onerous; we should live lightly on the earth.

Hence the implications in Levinas's thinking for Zionism. It's always going to be pretty contentious to argue that the Jewish people oughtn't to have a homeland, given the forced displacements and worse that they have suffered, nor does Levinas say anything so crude. Nevertheless the pathos for home involved in Zionism might give cause for suspicion. Why would it not lead to a defensiveness and an aggression toward outsiders that replicates the very situation that was being escaped? It's not just Israel, it's the founding of any state that identifies that state too strongly with being a fortress, that risks producing violence; a Palestinian state would be as prone to the same behavior. An exaggerated sense of belonging brings with it an exaggerated need to exclude. With land comes identity, and with identity come the borders around the self that define it as discrete, as impervious to the other, and, in the worst cases, as outwardly aggressive.

As for Zion itself, and the wider nexus of territories and buildings that concentrate around the spiritual home that is Jerusalem—spiritual home of Christians, Jews, and Muslims alike—perhaps the most interesting recent research on the subject has been conducted by the Christian theologian Margaret Barker. She argues that it's not just the sense of self—a self in opposition to an other—but whole religions that depend specifically on the place. Like individuals, religions need a home too, and they've often been forced to move house against their will. This raises the question of the difference between one's spiritual and one's actual home. One can't really dwell in a temple, no matter how devout one is. One might, however, spend a great deal of time attending to the "spirit" of one's home, its feel and general homeliness. This won't be quite the same as religious spirit, but it might mark a halfway house (literally) between one's residential address and preferred place of worship. Meanwhile that place of worship can exert a gravitational pull that makes people feel "at home" in a way that depends on the earth where it stands, as in Heidegger, but also provides a platform for communion with heaven.

For Barker, the original temple in Jerusalem, subsequently destroyed and rebuilt, provided a site for practicing religion, to be sure, but also determined how religious doctrine itself should work. If Jerusalem feels like the ultimate home for millions, it's because the physical architecture of the temple traced out a blueprint for faith. Specifically, the temple features an inner sanctum, or holy of holies, from which the temple extends forward. Access to this sacred shrine couldn't be more highly restricted, and hence, in Christianity at least, there is a need for some mediating force. This leads to the concept of nothing less than Jesus Christ, who functions as the great high priest, interceding between the Almighty, who presides in the holy of holies, and the worshipful multitude that gathers around.

In more everyday terms, the architecture of where we reside is more than incidental to our well-being, more than an empty structure for the spiritual actualization that might or might not proceed within. The design could be crucial. Yes, we construe *home* as a feeling, or even a spiritual state, but let's not let that diminish how the architectural character of the building might contribute. Obviously, in moving house one looks for such features—more light, extra space, better layout—but there's a broader sense in which the architecture contributes to this deep and pleasant sense of home. In other words, one can separate the concepts of house and home, but sooner or later they merge.

Given this relationship, the question then is, What should home be like? Ought it not reflect its occupants, so that they can feel more at home in it? If *home* is about familiarity, doesn't the homestead need to feel like us? We've grown accustomed to the idea that you can tell a lot about a person from his or her home—hence deciphering the contents of the moving van as your new neighbor arrives—and in childhood we draw pictures of home that stand as a metonym for the family that inhabits it. To be homely the house must be human or at least amenable to us anthropomorphizing it, a fact borne out precisely by those childhood drawings in which the house itself presents a "face" of sorts, with the windows as eyes, the door the nose or mouth, and the roof a hat. The homeliness of the archetypal home comes from it presenting literally a *façade* that we can recognize and respond to with familiarity and warmth—as if we were seeing ourselves.

Though the children's drawings remain unchanged and plenty of housing developers continue to throw up the low-risk vernacular cottage, the archetypal house might have been still more dominant today had it not been interrupted in the twentieth century by architects such as Le Corbusier, keen on rethinking domestic and other design. For Le Corbusier, the home couldn't be further from the *Heimat*-style folksy den of self-approval, and proposed itself instead as a "machine for living in." Homeliness might conceivably accrue to such houses in time, but might also obscure the naked fact that the home mainly had to serve a purpose. Compared with Heidegger's *dwelling*, Le Corbusier's *living* was a far more functional affair, which defined the human not in relationship to its passive and autochthonous Being but to its active need to carry out certain tasks, like cooking or washing. Built mostly from concrete rather than brick or wood, and uniformly white, these modern floating boxes brought an elegant severity to life at home, even as they pulled the notion of home up by the roots. The materials used meant they were often not organically related to the places where they were built, but imposed upon it, and gave off an international rather than a local air, suggesting that leaving them to move to another such house might be that much easier. What's more, the clean lines and harsh light called for cool, functional furniture and open-plan interiors, implicitly excluding the bric-a-brac that accumulates in a traditional home, and with it the personal history and homeliness such trivial objects betoken.

Indeed Le Corbusier sought explicitly to wipe the face off such buildings, that is, to remove the anthropomorphic façade of the house, but not out of trenchant antihumanism. His starting point was rather that the old-style house had had its design constrained by the fact that its exterior walls were load-bearing and so could tolerate only so many windows, thus limiting the light transfer from outside to inside. The gloominess of Victorian homes might make them snug, but also depressing, whereas light, which in Le Corbusier's day was particularly associated the alleviation of tuberculosis and health more generally, might actually improve one's quality of life at home. To liberate the outer walls, however, required some lateral thinking, literally. Le Corbusier proposed internal pillars to carry the weight of the house, and even to lift it off the ground. Along with wall-length horizontal windows and those pillars that made them possible, he advocated an often vacant ground floor without walls over which the mass of the building would hover, suggesting another kind of lightness.

Taken together, these innovations led to the construction of private homes that, though antiseptic to some, to many embodied a new ideal of beauty and a radical concept of what a house could be. This concept might seem cold, but the increased use of glass enabled closer, not more distant, connection with the surrounding land: from inside you could see more of the fields or trees, and from the outside your eye would be carried through to the inside on an uninterrupted sight line. This dissolving of the boundary between inside and outside might make its inhabitants feel more exposed, but at least visually it anchored them in the location, thus (pre)fabricating a truly modern model of Heideggerian belonging, despite the two men's different starting points.

But whether from a modernist box or a thatched cottage, the experience of moving out of one and into another nearly always brings stress, and not often because of the aesthetics of the buildings involved. If on the stressometer it scores alongside birth, death, and marriage, it's probably because so many divergent concerns converge on it. There's not only the sheer physicality of packing and shipping all your stuff and the accompanying risk of breakage; there's also the anxiety about the money involved, the bureaucratic niceties, the legal requirements, the personality of the real estate agent, and so on. Perhaps worst is the sheer uncertainty, for moving house typically means going somewhere new, somewhere untested, which makes the whole endeavor far more speculative than one would ever normally countenance. You really know what a house is like only by living in it, and unless by good fortune you've been staying in it for a while to test it out, you can't live in it until you live in it. In this it's like other milestones: you don't experience it until you experience it. But the peculiarity is that most homes we move into will have been occupied by someone else, whereas when we learn to talk, for example, nobody will have talked in our own body before us. Moving house usually means moving into what was, until that morning, somebody else's house.

Of course, our main concern when moving is not the previous owners but, on the contrary, what we're going to do with the place. The sense of project and possibility is uplifting, and one lies in bed in the weeks before moving thinking about which colors to paint which room and where to deploy the assorted but somehow complementary belongings one has accumulated. The canvas might not be quite blank, in the sense that all properties have their limitations to work within, and there's only so much money you'll have available to spend on it, but nevertheless moving house offers something exceptional: a place both to live in and to express yourself through. You get to live in an environment you've created, like stepping inside a painting.

Yet we're nearly always just one in a series of occupants of a given homestead, and the previous owners, wittingly or not, stand between us and our fully taking ownership of the new place. The very fact they were there first can't help but give them a kind of priority over the house, and it can take a while before the place feels like our own. At the basic level, moving out means taking your things away and leaving the property clean, but there's a symbolic or emotional aspect too, to do with the other kinds of baggage the previous owners left behind. At its least malign, these prior occupants might have lived a whole life in your new house, meaning that their metaphorical as well as literal dust will take time to settle. Perhaps an equation operates, like that for working out retirement packages, whereby for every year you've lived in a house, it takes a month for your presence in it to fade following your final departure. During this quarantine, the new owners can't quite take full possession of their new home, and their slightly nervous reaction to the house's strange noises on the first few nights is symptomatic of their unestablished legitimacy in it.

And there's real haunting. "Real" can be disputed, of course; we've still to acquire forensic evidence of houses being haunted, even if plenty of individuals who've seen a ghost, like those who've witnessed the Loch Ness monster, swear by their experience. Evidenced or not, there might nevertheless exist a negative version of the feeling of home-liness, namely "unhomeliness," the sense of being spooked in a particular place, especially an unfamiliar house we've recently moved into. The Germans have a literal term for this: *unheimlich*, which gets translated as *uncanny*. Precisely because they have hosted so much life, all houses are poten-tially uncanny in the sense that the life of those who lived there before can come back to life. In one's very home, the site of familiarity, there's the chance for the greatest strangeness. This is because hardly anything is so strange as people who've been there before you; they are stranger even than the strangers you've never met and who live else-where, because they leave behind an inscrutable trace and the faintest suggestion of still laying a claim to the land over which you, in the objective world, have established own-ership. In moving house, there's always this latent worry, that one is disturbing someone else's legacy and raking up ghosts that might otherwise have slept in peace.

15

Going Through
a Midlife Crisis

The simple fact that this chapter sits as the fifteenth of nineteen sheds light on its subject matter. As the table of contents shows, life's milestones tend to be front-loaded, clustering into the first third of one's days, which suggests that midlife crisis might partly be a response to life having run out of novelty. By the time you reach forty-five, say, it's highly likely you'll have done all the big things at least once, and there might not be a whole lot to look forward to. Except life's ending.

So perhaps the midlife crisis represents the guileless attempt, in the midst of unhappeningness, simply to make something happen. Yes, it will involve a resistance to or denial of getting older, but getting older wouldn't need to be resisted or denied if it promised the level of excitement and change experienced in youth. At the very least, the midlife crisis hopes to disrupt what later life might otherwise become: depressingly predictable. Which might explain why the crisis—buying a Porsche, running off with someone half one's age, buying a farm—can take such different forms.

The timing of the crisis is actually a symptom of modernity. Although it's always been possible, no matter one's life expectancy, to imagine that life divided in half, the phenomenon of living so long after having spawned and worked is relatively recent. In the Middle Ages you wouldn't have had the luxury of a midlife crisis: you'd be dead by forty. Today, however, if we live to a hundred and work until sixty, that leaves 40 percent of life without an easily defined or culturally determined shape. Like property developers who construct retirement homes but decline to build the shops or cinemas to complement them, science and technology have succeeded in prolonging our residency on earth without furnishing the points of interest to divert it. Chronologically, the crisis taking place in midlife might be accurate, but psychologically it marks not a point between two equal periods, but a radical asymmetry with, at its bleakest, almost everything in the first and, in the second, very slim pickings. For better or for worse, the relative paucity of events in the later stretches of life must make death appear nearer.

It's worth distinguishing, however, between the crisis itself and the reaction to it. When we bandy about the phrase *midlife crisis*, it's often jocular, but that crisis might represent a response to something altogether less risible, namely the creeping disquiet or lack of self-esteem that in one's middle years threatens to gather into a stagnant pool. The behavior should be understood as a symptom of a relatively serious malaise, and the Porsche as only an outer sign. If such examples are predominantly male, they have, in the signing-up for tummy tucks and the enlisting of boytoys, their female equivalents, also designed to resurrect a state of triumph. Indeed with age the gender stereotypes scarcely fade—conceivably they intensify—with middle-aged men striving again to be tigers and middle-aged women pussy-cats. But what unites both genders is precisely the nostalgia, for it's this that provides the antidote to that malaise's spreading presence.

As it happens, the *algia* part of the word *nostalgia* designates "pain," defining nostalgia as an experience more unpleasant than pleasant. This differs markedly from the modern understanding of nostalgia as the indulgence in mushy memories, going back as far as Homer's *Odyssey*, with its hero's yearning to be back in the arms of his beloved Penelope in Ithaca; the longer he has to wait, the more painful it gets. So although the midlife crisis might come with images of one's past that are consoling in the current sense of nostalgia, what makes it a crisis is that inside those images lurks something distressing. In effect, it stages a confrontation between one's older and one's younger self, with the former apologizing to the latter and begging for a second chance.

As ever, the best cure will be prevention, and in this we can get some help from Nietzsche. Because he spent his twilight years in a lunatic asylum, his advice on how to live one's life might not seem the most salutary, yet before he went mad he produced extraordinary insights about how to avoid the self-reproach that's become so characteristic of midlife crisis. This *self* is key. One of the more important aspects of the midlife crisis is that it involves self-reflection. The middle years almost demand a personal audit, an inventory of wins and losses; for those people unschooled in such introspection, the mere fact of looking inside oneself can bring on a crisis. Where previously your gaze settled on life's outer events, observing the phantasmagoria of things, now an inward bell tolls, urging you to examine the unexamined within. It can bring jarring surprises, like the realization that you might never be as sharp again, or that some relationships have irrecoverably withered. Nietzsche's point, however, is that you can begin the self-reflection earlier on, and thus preempt the great half-time catastrophe.

It's no accident that when, to coincide with his forty-fifth birthday, Nietzsche writes his own self-reflection, an autobiographical text called *Ecce Homo*, it exudes rampant self-celebration. The title, referring to Jesus Christ's declaration on the point of crucifixion, "Behold the man!," provides the first clue. Nietzsche wants to both compare and contrast himself with the Christian messiah. You might object that such megalomania counts among the surest signs of midlife crisis, but Nietzsche would say it's precisely the glorification of the self that Christianity exists to suppress. While Christ himself becomes the object of worship, the rest of us are required to abase ourselves, the necessary counterpart of his becoming so high being our bowing so low. Go into a typical church and you will see the cross raised up above the altar and the heads of the faithful worshipfully bent; in some ceremonies the priest will literally lie on the floor face down in abasement. Christianity, in Nietzsche's view, practices a sinister ideology designed to make slaves of us in the name of humility. Indeed Christian morality takes as its principal aim a psychological castration whereby our lack of worth is first imposed upon us and then redescribed as a virtue. It's good to be humble, says Christianity. That's just to make us weak so the institution of the Church in all its pomp can profit from it, Nietzsche retorts.

This suppression of the self suggests in turn that it is mankind rather than Christ who harbors the true potential for extraordinary works, which provides a glimpse of an exit from midlife crisis. Could we but cast the Christian or moralistic scales from our eyes, Nietzsche implores, we would even see ourselves as gods—though clearly not in the Christian vein. The key thing is turning religious passivity into secular activity. You do this by asserting your will and refusing to let things like mortgage, marriage, and work wear you down. For these quotidian fetters barely differ from the moralistic ones; in both cases, one can end up living a very small existence. By exerting one's will, however, one can break out; one can even release the "antichrist" within, the closet hero we all are, now unbound by any doctrine of senseless humility and religious stupefaction.

So what is this *will* that so potently explodes the path that descends to midlife crisis? Again, the self lies at its heart: the unbendable intent to posit oneself, or to *individuate*. That means being highly wary of joining any group, for example, for groups easily become like flocks of sheep who follow each other dumbly. Instead the self resolves into a unique unit that decides upon and then implements its own destiny. But you can't just start individuating. First you must believe, *contra* some Christian theology, that the world hasn't been predetermined and that enough undecided space exists in the future for you to mold it according to your own particular vision. The same world needs to be understood as radically open, as lacking the capacity we often ascribe to it of resisting one's will, of issuing impediments and inhibitions to one's progress. Only then can we fall into our expansive freedom.

How far this Nietzschean ideal lies from the typical midlife crisis, which at best can parody such efforts of self-overcoming! When the paunchy man in his forties buys an electric guitar, he may well be nursing an inner vision of himself as a rock god still to be admired, but such belated gestures at personal redemption belong squarely to a type—nothing individual about them at all. Just as when he was a teenager he had the cool but no money, he's now got the money to buy a top-of-the-line Gibson, but he's lost his cool, and with it his spark of difference. A properly Nietzschean crisis would involve becoming less, not more, generic in one's aspirations. Insofar as it prepares the self for a moment of rupture, the *crisis* part of the ordinary midlife crisis might be very good, but if it functions merely as the prelude to regression, very bad. Advancement is the thing.

But if advancement matters so much, why not derive it, if not from religion per se, at least from the realm of the soul? Whereas the worst midlife crisis takes the form of plucking things out of one's youth and inserting them into the current aged reality, like a hair transplant, the best involves realizing that one can't simply repeat or replicate. Indeed though crisis can be unsettling, it can lead to the mature recognition that the values that have served you so far will not do for the future. If the first twenty years or so were dominated by biological change, education, and romantic questing, and the next by the need to establish oneself in the world, then the midlife crisis has the merit of holding that world at arm's length and interrogating its expectations and exigencies. As a turning away from life rather than further into it, midlife crisis differs from other milestones like taking exams or getting a job, encouraging you instead to resist the very road that has its milestones so implacably stationed along the way. Do I really want to keep going along with the rat race? Is getting promoted really so important? Does the city really have the edge over the country? And so on. Simply by putting mental clear water between oneself and one's context, some of the unfreezing of the soul necessary for potential movement will have been effected.

We find the most famous example of this midlife stirring of the soul in Dante's *The Divine Comedy*, the early fourteenth-century Italian poem that opens:

> *Midway life's journey I was made aware*
> *That I had strayed into a dark forest,*
> *And the right path appeared not anywhere.*

The setup couldn't be simpler, and yet it contains extraordinary richness and says a lot about the spiritual dimension of midlife crisis. Once you've settled down—bought a house or gotten married or had kids or found regular work or all of the above—habit takes over. Now your routine does the work for you, without you having to think. What's more, that routine's defining absence of change produces fewer signs demarcating the distance traveled, and so time appears to accelerate. Taken together, these conditions make it likely that you will not only sleepwalk in a direction you never quite intended, but that you'll do so ever faster. Until you arrive in a dark forest.

From Greek myths through Shakespeare's Arden to German fairy tales and beyond, forests have been associated with confusion and the vulnerability that goes with it. In the chapter on starting school I mentioned their potential for savagery. Whereas in the town, reason, order, and light will reign, out in the forest all recedes into an impenetrable gloom in which one might lose, if not one's life, then perhaps one's money, virtue, mind, or soul. Of these, it is the last to which Dante's lines allude. The allusiveness has a special intent: those trees visually echo the columns in a church, and the poem as a whole will reach a climax with a picture of the divine light streaming through a rose window. So although the forest thickens into darkness and danger, it also hints at possible illumination, safety, and even rapture. For now, however, midway life's journey, darkness prevails with a pall that belongs as much to the inner mind of the traveler as the outer world of the forest.

Fortunately a new awareness has arisen. If beforehand you were somnambulating through your life, now you are shaken awake. What you observe on waking may be dismal, but at least you have gained a cognizance of it, and so, in principle, you can act. Had the stumbling through the forest gone on much longer, the way out might never have been found, the deviation too large to correct. More promisingly still, a "right path" somewhere exists. For now it's lost, but what makes midlife a crisis rather than a tragedy is that the path may yet be refound. Dante's Italian has *la diritta via*, which can also be translated as "the true way" or "the direct way," and these too carry religious overtones. While *via* enjoys a perfectly literal existence as a road— such as the Via Appia, the ancient highway heading out of Rome that Dante would likely have known—it enjoyed in the theology of the age a special metaphorical place as the road to God. A *via* was a way of being, and thus a true path that might be more conducive to divine connection. Very easy to get waylaid in the forest of human uncertainty, but not impossible to navigate back to a path that implicitly takes you beyond humanity altogether and on toward that refulgent light.

In Dante, the forest symbolizes spiritual distortion, whereas in modern terms the escape from the city might hold the forest or the countryside as its destination—precisely because it's the *city* that swarms with the consumerist infestations so noxious to one's spiritual health. Take Henry David Thoreau's *Walden*; published in 1850s America with the subtitle *A Life in the Woods*, this was the record of Walden's own midlife crisis and his experiment with living away from the town. The work celebrates the ideal of getting back to nature, where getting back to nature and rejoining one's spiritual path have, rightly or wrongly, often been conflated. Whether the forest is good, as in Thoreau, or bad, as in Dante, what matters is that the midlife crisis acts as a spur to disinter a true self that, thanks to the pressure of daily life, has got buried. This true self will always rank higher in the spiritual chain of being than the outer, public self we've developed around it like a husk.

All this talk of the soul, however, might feel a little indulgent when we remember that the principal manifestations of midlife center on the body. Although it's plausible that we age at a constant rate, it feels like the process moves in steps. A first gray hair is a first gray hair, not a gradual tingeing. Nor does the process affect men and women in the same way. Yes, the phrase *midlife crisis* might conjure images of helpless men before those of hapless women, but this doesn't mean the female version of the crisis lacks specificity. On the contrary, if one goes by the work of Germaine Greer on the subject, this moment of midlife reconfiguring for women, in the form of "the change," has particular properties that culturally we remain a long way from recognizing.

This is because at least two taboos hover around the

middle-aged and menopausal woman: middle age and menopause. In Western culture at least, a man will be allowed to grow old, and it doesn't have to be gracefully for his silver sideburns to be commended as "distinguished." Even if he lets himself go, he'll have set his store more by his worldly achievements than his physical appearance, and these generally outlast the body's incorrigible sagging and wilting. Women, by contrast, who are culturally required to lead with their looks, will all too often find their stock depleted when their physical being starts to tarnish. Age works more against women, and in Greer's analysis, it cloaks them with a pervasive invisibility. The flipside of the fixation held by both men and women with young attractive females is an almost complete disregard for women beyond their so-called prime.

Menopause hardly helps. Just as society dictates that women must be young, so they must be fertile. Again men, who never lose their capacity to sire children, have the better deal. The midlife crisis might bring on in him the odd bout of sexual impotence, but relative to the woman's less reversible loss of fecundity, that's perhaps not as drastic as it might appear in the moment. Being fertile enjoys all sorts of positive associations with health and abundance, whereas *menopause* gives off a dour and forbidding feel. True, we can joke about menopause and hot flashes, and the humor goes some way toward mitigating the anxiety we experience, but from the Greer perspective, the physical fact of menopause gets too quickly translated into an emotional sense that women of a certain age have moved beyond what was their zenith. If our culture praises lithe and bountiful maidens, then by definition the postmenopausal woman will find it harder to be noticed, let alone afforded significant status. Clearly that's a loss as much to society as to the particular woman whose other attributes—greater experience or wisdom, for example—will get neglected into the bargain.

At about the same time the children this woman may have had, and who will have provided living testament of her erstwhile fertility, will themselves be fleeing the nest, meaning that the woman's self-image as mother gets doubly shaken. Like her male counterpart, she remains a parent, but now it's a case of parenting at a distance, a hands-off care for the young ones that can mix up the emotions. It's wonderful seeing the kids make their own future, but after all, the mother was once the most needed figure in those kids' lives, and no longer being needed can disclose a great emptiness. Mom and Dad turn to each other and experience the strange sensation of being a couple again, but now in a house they rattle around in and with an inkling that, following the departure of their children, life happens elsewhere. Yet this critical phase, like the shedding of a skin, can create a new sense of possibility. So long as the midlife crisis avoids those traps of nostalgia, of regression and regret, it can wipe the slate clean for a rebeginning.

16

Getting Divorced

When studying history, every English schoolchild of my generation had to learn the following rhyme:

> *Divorced, beheaded, died;*
> *Divorced, beheaded, survived.*

No prizes for knowing that this mnemonic pertains to the serial monogamist monarch Henry VIII and his luckless wives. Frustrated by the lack of male issue to continue the Tudor line, he cast off wife after wife with varying degrees of pity, barely pausing to consider that the cause might lie behind the magnificent codpiece worn so ostentatiously by his royal self.

You might think that compared with beheading and death, divorce sounds innocuous, but its historical import is significant, and it helps explain why, despite its increasing prevalence, divorce retains a modicum of stigma. Henry couldn't just get divorced; he had to restructure the entire religious system in order to do so. Born a Roman Catholic, he was answerable on religious matters to the pope and upward to the Lord himself, both of whom had expressly forbidden divorce. If he needed corroboration, it was there in the Bible, with Matthew relating the story of the Pharisees quizzing Jesus on the matter:

> "Haven't you ever read," he replied, "that at the beginning the Creator 'made them male and female,' and said, 'For this reason a man will leave his father and his mother and be united to his wife, and the two will become one flesh'? So they are no longer two, but one. Therefore, what God has joined together, let no man separate."

Faced with dogma of such adamantine strength, Henry chose the nuclear option. Rather than languishing in a fruitless marriage but keeping in good with the pope, he broke away from Rome entirely and took a wreckling ball to most of the Catholic monasteries in England into the bargain. The price of divorce was a rift in the Christian Church and a personal risk to Henry that, having scorned the scripture, he might not make it to heaven. Except now that he was master of his own religion, he could make up the rules. So divorce was made legal, and all could proceed according to his formidable will.

You don't have to be a Catholic to sense that this aggressive intervention might have done damage to the institution of marriage, or that divorce might carry something unholy about it. After all, marriage is meant to last for life, so even if you marry outside a religious edifice, the idea of terminating that marriage might well feel like a violation. Marriage vows aren't sworn lightly, so in most cases reneging on them ushers in a commensurate pang of conscience. On the other hand, Henry cleared the path for all and sundry behind him—not just vainglorious potentates with a royal need to reproduce, but ordinary souls who'd gotten hitched in good faith but found themselves many years on in loveless or abusive relationships that would have otherwise locked them in. In this sense, divorce offered a merciful means of reclaiming a quantum of personal liberty in the face of what might have been drudgery til death do us part.

But we're jumping ahead. That notion of divorce as the restoration of freedom or the escape from unhappiness would need several hundred years to mature. A century after Henry's high-stakes démarche, John Milton, the not unwilling inheritor of anti-Roman skepticism, was still publicly struggling with the rightness of divorce, which he too sought to justify. Like Henry's, his arguments disguised a personal motive—he'd been jilted by a new bride—but were aggrandized with social and religious portent.

Milton took more seriously, or at least more cerebrally, the need to find a rapprochement between divorce and Holy Writ, and published a handful of sinuously argued tracts aimed at dissolving the apparently overwhelming contradiction between what Jesus had stipulated and what Milton himself proposed. As in *Paradise Lost*, he was struggling to reconcile the complexity of human behavior with the simplicity of divine injunction. In fact his portrayal of the relationship in that great epic poem between Adam and Eve pretty much captured what marriage should look like: "the apt and cheerful conversation of man with woman, to comfort and refresh him against the evils of solitary life." Ergo the waning of these conditions could, to Milton, justify the move to divorce.

At first blush, this Miltonic picture of marital bliss does seem modern. His seventeenth-century coreligionists would have held the drier, more doctrinal view that marriage existed mainly to suppress fornication and release offspring, whereas Milton is picturing a warm cohabitation of adults, even if the equality implied in that gets undermined by the woman appearing to pander to the man. But while marriage, for Milton, should be a unique communion of two human beings pursuing earthly contentment, that doesn't mean such terrestrial serenity escapes the eyes of God. Milton's modernity went only so far. This felicitous intercourse of man and woman remained framed by a larger devotion to the Almighty, the one who had bestowed the great gift of marriage upon mankind in the first place. A happy marriage thus offered a means of glorifying God. Conversely, to Milton an unsuccessful marriage implied a limit not just on the happiness of the couple, but on the potentially divine nature of their union. Rather than being sinful or at least irreligious, divorce therefore represented an honest, if expedient, means of exiting a relationship that itself threatened to become not only unhappy, but, in its very discord, ungodly.

Not that divorce marks the end of the matter. By invoking the "evils of the solitary life," Milton seems to suggest that marriage represents the nobler state, and from this we, with our modern attitudes, could infer that divorce should be deployed as a device not just for ending but for transitioning between relationships. After all, the divorcee becomes as solitary as the singleton, subject to evils, whatever they may be, on a comparable scale. Better if possible to regain paradise, to get back to that Edenic ideal where the albeit unequal discourse between man and woman enacts a freedom of the mind, this being the very condition of happiness. What's evil about the solitary life of the divorcee is, among other things, the deficit in this human interchange, the lack of mental exercise that comes from having nobody with whom to debate. Divorce might provide a useful, and not ignoble, segue out of misery, but until converted into a new and more wholesome marriage, it threatens to slide into its own slough of despond.

In this particular sense, the stigma of divorce remained undissolved, just as today no one actually prefers divorce to marriage, at least in principle. But perhaps it's a question of distinguishing between divorce as this short-term way out of an ill-fated liaison and the long-term condition of ruefulness, between getting divorced and being divorced, between an act and a mode. Generally the stigma applies more to the latter, whereby being a divorcee suggests something, if not toxic, a little off-putting: bundled up with the final divorce papers, you get a public, legal label that marks you as having failed in marriage—even if it wasn't your fault—and that's not much of an attractor. What's more, because there's no divorce without marriage, the state of being divorced must always stand in relation to the past, meaning the divorcee by definition carries baggage, and this encumbers him or her in the task of mixing with the present. To fraternize with divorcees is to be presented with the mystery of their background, with the enigma of the marriage that collapsed, and with the question of how far they remain in a union that legally has released but psychologically has detained them.

So much for the *mode* of being divorced. By contrast, the *act* of divorce sounds short and sharp, but the reality rarely yields such neatness. "Acrimonious," "messy," "expensive," "dragging on"—such is the lexicon that hangs in divorce's gray and gloomy tag cloud. Like it or not, divorce is a process, and a process that can take on a life of its own. The reasons aren't hard to identify: two people who can't agree and are trying to part are forced together to agree how to part, egged along in their grievances by lawyers who, charging by the hour, have scant interest in hastening matters to a conclusion. Precisely because of the legalistic emphasis on competing claims, the divorce process is set up to repeat or exacerbate the very dynamic that in many cases led to the marriage's demise. Those claims may now be more financial than emotional, but they tend to follow similar contours, not least because money and feelings often function as a proxy for each other. Moreover, as the academic lawyer Stephen Cretney points out, divorce by consent of the two parties without the intervention of a court is still a long way off: divorce can't be practiced independent of that formidable machinery. If the marriage rate has been steadily declining, it surely has as much to do with the practical avoidance of this potential outcome as the principled rejection of marriage as an institution. If you only live together, you only need to part—you don't need a divorce.

Besides, splitting up from a partner rather than a spouse can be done in private, whereas divorce, like marriage itself, has become grand theater. The fact that it's legal already lends divorce an inherently public aspect that's only been further burnished thanks to a series of high-profile marital meltdowns. From King Edward and Wallis Simpson through Prince Charles and Lady Diana and on to the Hollywood bust-ups of so-called celebrities, one follows divorces in the media as if they were a genre of entertainment. Divorce could be the modern version of Greek tragedy, the public acting-out of the private antagonism between VIPs whose travails are nevertheless as fascinatingly familiar as our own. And whereas in Greek tragedy it's death that's guaranteed in advance to scupper the splendor and complacence of the royal household, so today fate decrees that pretty much any high-rolling marriage will end in tears. It's what one expects, and, most obligingly, couple after glamorous couple will be dividing up the wedding gifts within a few years of wedded woe.

Such divvying up hardly gets easier when there are children involved. Their presence complicates the already challenging disentanglement of assets where prenups don't apply or the dependent partner expects to be kept in the manner to which he or she has become accustomed. Just as there's a more or less explicit dowry on both sides upon getting wed—houses, cars, stocks—upon divorce there's the intricate parceling out of capital, which, in itself somewhat sordid, has the bonus feature of grimly adumbrating the disbursement of one's estate at death. Taking things back out of the shared pot never feels as good as putting them in, for assets, like people, are better combined, more likely to secure compound benefit for those who have invested. That said, if children count as assets they belong to a different order.

Memorably, the poster for the 1979 Oscar-winning film *Kramer vs. Kramer* pictured an ideal family of three: Dad hugging Mom and both thereby making the securest possible framework for their cherubic son, Billy. Memorable because of its irony: the film was to show the child tugged between its two divorcing parents during a protracted and insufferable court case. Memorable too, of course, for the bold perversity of the title, *Kramer vs. Kramer*. Here was not husband *and* wife, this being the natural order of things, but husband *against* wife—spousal strife, as cosmologically wrong and self-defeating as cannibalism or civil war. The symmetry of the two names, Kramer and Kramer, thus worked as a verbal trompe l'oeil, with the eye deceived into perceiving a harmony—don't forget, the wife has taken the husband's very name as a token of affinity—whereas it's not harmony but hostility that prevails. The *v* of *vs.* visually alludes to a seesaw and the power balance between the former lovers, the deeper irony being that Billy himself shares the name and yet can find no place.

What the fearful symmetry of the title *Kramer vs. Kramer* disguises, however, is that, children or no, each party in a divorce starts from a different position. Again the legal construct makes matters worse, now by positioning one as *petitioner*, the other as *respondent*, or, to put it baldly, an innocent and a guilty party. It begins with the perfectly incontestable point that, for a divorce to be granted, there need to be grounds: you shouldn't get divorced on a whim. Admittedly you can obtain a quickie divorce in Las Vegas as readily as a wedding, but if that's the case, then between the marriage's start and finish a parity of seriousness obtains, and perhaps there's your rule. The more earnest the wedding vows, the graver the divorce needs to be. Graver too the charges, the "grounds" that need to be laid. It might not be a criminal proceeding, but the reasonable requirement to adduce grounds and evidence ratchets the ante up to a level that falls only so far short. While most marriages break down for a mass and a mess of emotional reasons, the courts lack a mechanism for dealing with such intangibles, and so look for quasi-criminal grounding in quaint-sounding but at least measurable factors like "adultery" or one partner being "not of sound mind." Such language manufactures an injustice to which the court can now pedantically respond. Meanwhile, in the form of sheer incompatibility, the injustice will long have been experienced by the unhappy couple as emotional blight. They know all too well that any "symmetry" in the relationship will have been compromised well before the legal machinery confirmed it.

Fortunately many legal systems are waking up to such truths and considering new measures to compensate. Not least because of a belated recognition of the preeminent needs of the victim, that is, the child, they are attempting to remind us, against the cultural tide, that divorce isn't an escape clause engraved invisibly into any marriage contract, but an option strictly of last resort. They would far rather symmetry and harmony be restored, thus precluding the need to come to court. To that end, counseling and reconciliation services have been gathering like paralegals around the legalities. Besides, if divorce is a process, it doesn't proceed straight from marital discontent to the hiring of attorneys; in most cases there will be an attempt, no matter how half-hearted, to "save the marriage," and this will often mean hiring a different sort of professional, namely a therapist, albeit with a similar hourly rate.

Hence the rise of couples therapy. Adapted from personal therapy and psychoanalysis, it has the obvious difference that two clients rather than one sit before the presiding shrink. *Presiding* alludes to judges, of course, and among the many oddities of couples therapy is that although expressly designed to forestall the need for legal divorce proceedings, the dynamic clearly resembles a scene in which competing attorneys make their case before a judge. Husband and wife will find it hard not to try, even if subconsciously, to win over the therapist. The therapist meanwhile must do everything in her power to resist, for it's the very absence of judgment that facilitates the therapeutic mood. By setting aside judgment and blame, the skilled therapist helps the couple in turn to remove the lens of grievance through which they view their problem, and thus makes it possible, in theory, for each to stand in the other's shoes. Where the couple in crisis will see all in terms of difference, the therapist, by enabling such empathy between them, hopes to conjure instead the sameness that enticed the couple to couple in the first place.

If that sounds like a skill, wait until you introduce transference. First schematized by Freud, *transference—Übertragung* in German—names the emotional static that builds up when patient addresses therapist. You don't talk to your therapist as you talk to a friend; the neutrality that the therapist achieves simply through being independent, and which she will have perfected through such techniques as suspending judgment, means that the therapist becomes a blank background on which the patient paints whatever portrait suits. Physically she's a therapist, but emotionally she changes shape to become the patient's mother, sister, enemy, friend, or any combination thereof. Not that absolute neutrality on the therapist's part can ever really be attained—she's only human—resulting in cross-currents back to the patient, known artlessly as *countertransference*. The upshot is that both patient and therapist are each talking to another person in the room who is only in part who they really are and is just as much made up of fantasy. And that's just one-to-one therapy. Now introduce a third element, the patient's spouse, and you have a veritable pinball of transferential relays among the three, of which the therapist simultaneously needs to be mindful.

Can it ever work? Well, beneath the dizzying permutations runs a simple line of common sense: it's good to talk. If couples therapy, like psychoanalysis, is known as a "talking cure," it's not only because talking might obviate the need for more invasive action, like pharmaceuticals or divorce. It's also because failure of communication between husband and wife is what so often will have put the marriage under strain. Simply providing neutral territory and a time for the couple to hold a conversation thus goes a long way in defusing the divorce-oriented tension. To be more precise, good couples therapy fosters as much listening and talking, wherein lies a third technique the therapist will deploy: *reflecting back*. It might sound easy-peasy, but when a therapist echoes out loud what the husband, for example, has just said, it can have quite an effect. When the wife has got into the habit of listening to her spouse in a narrow way that filters what he says to fit with long-established prejudices about him, hearing his words from another's mouth can help her see that husband in a new light. If the therapist then goes further, and uses technique number four, known as *reframing*, further insights may follow. Reframing involves taking what the patient says and restating it in a way that discloses the underlying emotion. For example, the husband claims, "My wife doesn't understand me," and the therapist says, "You don't feel understood." The therapist thus turns an objective accusation about the wife, one likely to provoke retaliation, into a subjective sentiment more likely to induce sympathy and understanding.

The larger point, beyond all such techniques, must be that although divorce has infected our culture to the degree that it can find its place in this very book as one of life's predictable milestones, it's no error to see it as an aberration. Better therefore to nip marital strife in the bud. Whether you can imagine Henry VIII and Catherine of Aragon in couples therapy might be a moot point, but who knows: had it been available to them, the whole history of divorce, let alone the Christian Church, might have gone a different way.

17

Retiring

"To think, when one is no longer young, when one is not yet old, that one is no longer young, that one is not yet old, that is perhaps something." So writes Samuel Beckett in his work of prose fiction, *Watt*. Whether you find it bafflingly simple or simply baffling, it could serve as a motto for retirement. This is because although one associates retiring with getting old, it's not quite the same thing, even if one is no longer young. Retirement covers that fuzzy zone between being no longer young and not yet old, which is why there's a chapter following this one, called "Living the Third Age," that makes no bones about being wrinkly. To refer to your being retired after the age of eighty, say, will sound odd because it's pretty obvious that you would be. *Retirement* points much more to that first decade or so after giving up work, when one is no longer young but not yet old. Which is perhaps something.

It's precisely the giving up of work that defines retirement: you can't retire if you don't have a job to retire from. It's a milestone omitted by the idle rich, the long-term unemployed, the insane, the infirm, and kept women—demographic groups seldom otherwise connected. For them, life just carries on. For the majority, meanwhile, retiring is a rite of passage as predictable as was leaving school, with the caveat that where leaving school was a departure to gear up for entry into the world, retiring is a gearing down and a shuffling away. As the etymology of the word suggests, *to retire* is to pull back from something, to withdraw. Professional boxers, along with soccer players, racing drivers, and tennis players, will routinely hang up their boots, gloves, or rackets, but they don't count. No matter how many Wimbledon trophies you've amassed, to announce your retirement with your hair still thick and your muscles supple is a trifle disingenuous: you're still unambiguously young. Besides, for most sports stars, retirement heralds a new career as commentator, coach, or clotheshorse for multinational brands. Proper retirement, by my definition, means you'll never form part of the labor force again. It has to involve a final farewell.

In this moment of valediction, you will be saying goodbye to an occupation that, like it or loathe it, will have defined you for decades. Think of how you introduce yourself at parties: apart from your name, it's the question of what you do that will perhaps most exercise your interlocutor. Up until the day you retire, you can say you're the ventriloquist, bomb disposal expert, or yacht designer that you demonstrably are. But from the morning after, you may murmur no more than "I used to be an *X*." Having to refer back like this might sound pathetic—a trading on past glories—but there's little alternative: just saying you're retired doesn't carry the necessary weight, not least because *retiree* isn't an occupation, by definition. Though many will embrace the freedom that retirement brings and celebrate the loosing of the bonds of labor, there's a price to pay: surrendering a substantial part of one's identity and having to refer to it in the past tense.

Take the novel by John Lanchester, *Mr. Phillips*, in which the middle-aged hero loses the accountancy job that's so defined him. This is forced retirement as redundancy. When in the following days he beats the streets, he can't help but see the world through an accountant's eyes. Browsing at a newsstand, he notices the top-shelf magazines, and instead of being titillated by the salacious images he makes a calculation as to the financial basis of the porn industry, based on the number of women photographed per magazine, its likely circulation, the demand for new glamour models, the supply chain that delivers them, and so on. Numbers run through his blood. He simply *is* an accountant, whether in gainful employment or not.

What Mr. Phillips demonstrates is that although a job can come to an end, the skills acquired to perform it remain at hand. Even well into retirement the competencies you've honed—as publisher, mechanic, beautician, rope maker, general manager, nurseryman—may well find themselves without a use, and yet your capability to exercise them won't necessarily have dwindled. Hence people "coming out of retirement" to fill a vacancy that can't for the moment be staffed; hence too the option in retirement of still turning your skills to good use in other ventures.

The management guru Charles Handy has an interesting take on this question of skills. He points out that because the notion of a "job for life" is gradually being replaced by portfolio careers, one will increasingly find oneself at arm's length from any given organization, working as a freelancer or part time, for example. Retiring from a single job, or even a single profession, will only get rarer, and the question of losing your identity correspondingly complex. If you were several people during your working life, are you saying goodbye to all of them? Perhaps you are, but at least you'll still have those carefully built-up skills, and it may be these that define you more than any particular job you've held. This has to be a good thing, because it implies that having retired you can still deploy such skills to earn extra money or just get out the house. It also suggests that retirement itself will come to resemble those freelance lifestyles where you dip in and out of work, in which case you never fully retire, you just reduce the number of hours you put in across a wide range of activities.

There's a physical aspect to all this. Over the course of a working life your body will have learned to move in a certain pattern: getting in and out of the taxi you drive, leaning at a particular angle to cut someone's hair, holding your head up to watch the stocks sink or soar on the monitor. Such manifestations will be more obvious in the elongated neck of one-time ballet dancers or the mountainous stance of the ex-bouncer than in the lawyer or checkout clerk, but they apply to all. The haleness and heartiness in the farmer's demeanor will be lacking in the wax-skinned and stooped academic. Job identity even leaves its mark on the body.

The irony is that in continuing to exercise his algorithmic mind, Mr. Phillips doesn't let his identity flop—he actually maintains it. Like scaffolding, the job has been taken away, but the man still stands. Accountancy for him is the equivalent of having served in the armed forces or the church, where it's perfectly acceptable to be known as Captain Thingummy or Cardinal Whatsit long after you wind down. Similarly, ex-presidents of the USA remain "Mr. President." It's a practice that plausibly can be traced back to the medieval doctrine of the king's two bodies, as described by E. H. Kantorowicz, the German Jewish historian (and former Princeton professor). Though the Middle Ages had no concept of retirement, the king was considered both a person and a title, a living body and an office that would endure. Presidents are not monarchs, to be sure, but in a republic they're the closest you can get, and so to declare, long after you've retired from the Oval Office and Obama has been sworn in, that you're President Bush is to make a claim about the persistence and inviolability of the title. Actually this is somewhat different from taking your identity from a job and being able to prolong it: it's more that the job itself is immortal. For a retired president to be known as president is to affirm the dignified permanence of the position, regardless of the individual who has held it. The person retires, but the job never does.

So much for outgoing presidents. There's a less elevated category of worker whose identity upon retirement won't be effaced: those whose job is a vocation. Even the unassuming Mr. Phillips effectively made accountancy a vocation rather than a job, and it's this that allowed him, upon retirement, to become an accountant-without-portfolio, so to speak. But I'm also thinking back to the distinction made in an earlier chapter between getting a job and having a vocation. Aging painters remain painters, no matter their level of output, and vicars continue to be reverend. The truth is that, their work being a vocation, they never really retire from it; they keep going until they give out. Is that a blessing or a curse?

Whichever it is, they find themselves unprotected by the buffer that retirement seems to put in place against the Grim Reaper's surging onrush. In fact prior to retirement becoming established in the twentieth century, you would have chopped until you dropped or slaved until you caved anyway, meaning there was no difference between those with a vocation and those without. Carrying on until, paintbrush or shovel in hand, you keeled over on the job was the way of the world. From this perspective, the relatively modern arrival of retirement appears like a gift—one that grants, for however limited a period, the opportunity to enjoy some leisure before the body grows too frail. It's a marvelous invention.

This isn't to say that retirement can't actually hasten one's demise. As the actor Ernest Borgnine said, age ninety-three and on his way to shoot a movie with Bruce Willis, "Retirement will kill you, work gives you purpose." Much as you might focus on the classic three *G*s of retirement—golf, grandchildren, and galleries—the fact that they are discretionary activities suggests they might not add up to the sense of purpose you derived from work or produce the satisfaction of a job well done. Retirement pastimes might serve as a proxy for the real jobs they've superseded, but they don't require you to engage with the world in the same way. Working usually means being exposed to difference and to challenge, which is strengthening. Retirees tend to associate with other retirees, whereas workers will have colleagues with different opinions, backgrounds, ages, and ambitions. Surely mixing with such diversity would be good for the general well-being of sexagenarians, it would keep them on their toes, tuned in to different idioms and ideas. Perhaps the trick in retirement is not to retire: give up work if you must, but throw yourself into new and interesting situations. It's these that might help you to live beyond your expiry date. As Alexis de Tocqueville put it, "It is especially at this age that one cannot survive on what one has already learned but must attempt to learn more."

All this assumes that retirement will continue—an assumption worth testing. As a world we've developed such techniques of efficiency that it's possible to believe the balance between production and consumption can keep tilting toward the latter. But that has to be an illusion. Think of the exponential growth in the world's population I cited in the chapter on having children: that must have an impact. If retirement is a luxury afforded by societies so affluent they're capable of supporting a workforce after it's ceased working, then a decline in such affluence must lead to a proportional bearing down on retirement. In some countries the deletion of a compulsory retirement age has already happened. This era of retirement, at once so recent, may well prove ephemeral, and the idea of slipping into a "second childhood" could read in the future as a historical blip.

This pressure in the economic climate is bound to make us revisit the logic with which retirement has for so long been defended: you've put plenty of effort in, so you're entitled to take something out. Why shouldn't you be looked after in your twilight years? Robust enough at one level, there are philosophical as well as economic reasons for treating that logic with caution. Most apposite is the thinking of Bert Hellinger, a German philosopher and therapist, which insists on the importance of give-and-take in getting social systems to function. A Hellingerian argument might go as follows. Reaping the rewards of retirement after a life of work and paying your taxes sounds perfectly defensible until you factor in the support you received as a child. Before you even started in employment you drew on the state in some form or other: child benefits, public education, subsidized health care, free transport, not to mention discounted access to theme parks, leisure centers, museums, and zoos. If the three main phases of life are growing up, working, and retiring, you'll have been mollycoddled for two of those three. By the time you retire you'll have already used up a great deal of credit, and the balance of give-and-take will be out of whack. Better to say that all that tax you paid was to settle your childhood debts, as opposed to funding your retirement. The more equitable policy would be to keep working and try to be less of a burden on others. But as ever, the figures can be manipulated. Analyze the same problem using the unit of actual years and the graph considerably changes. You spent, say, twenty years growing up, forty working, and another twenty retiring. That adds up to forty giving and forty taking. It's a perfect balance, and Hellinger would be pleased—as long as when you hit eighty you either kill yourself or start applying again for jobs.

It's not the relationship to the state, however, but the relationship to the family that most preoccupies the retiree. A cliché it may be, but the prospect that retirement affords of "spending more time with the family" remains compelling. Where working life tended to get in the way of family togetherness, being retired means having quality time with relatives, especially grandchildren. Trying to identify what it is that makes him happy, John Updike writes in his memoirs, "A visit from my daughter and son-in-law and two grandsons was scheduled for that afternoon. I take an idle aesthetic delight in my grandsons I was too busy to spare my children, except when they were asleep."

For most retired grandparents the delight isn't just aesthetic, of course; it's the feeling of being connected, just as one's own old age is creeping up, with such unbounded youth. Apart from the equally clichéd thought that being a grandparent features all the gain and none of the pain of being a parent—which is partly what Updike is saying—being around one's grandchildren is to see life itself affirmed. There's a profound satisfaction in observing life having flowed through one's own children into theirs, and for it to be so wheelingly joyous.

Given this bountiful sensation, it's perhaps surprising that some people choose to retire overseas, that is, as far from family as can be. The lure of a Mediterranean climate, say, just can't be ignored. If your working life has been one of drudgery, then such warmth is the least compensation one might expect, so screw giving anything more back to the state. And if one already conceives of retirement as a metaphorical paradise, why not make the metaphor literal? There are plenty of TV shows featuring a place in the sun that encourage us to do just that. Retirement becomes the perpetual holiday we imagined it might be, picture postcard perfect.

Needless to say, the reality doesn't always match the vision, and those same TV shows have hatched a subgenre in which the reporter returns a year later to see how the retirees are getting on. Landing at Malaga Airport in January with the sea gray, the breeze harsh, and the restaurants closed for winter, said reporter walks with a knowingly false jauntiness up to the front door. Diane and Dave open up, and it's immediately apparent from their tanned but haggard faces that things haven't worked out as expected. They don't speak the lingo, find the local bureaucracy daunting, and never get invited to neighborhood shindigs. Yes, their time together has increased, but this isn't without its downsides; and yes, they've made friends with other expats, but most of their conversation tends to be about life back home. Above all they miss their family. The grandchildren have been out for a visit, but having to say goodbye to them when they left really tore at the heartstrings.

So this relationship to family upon retiring needs to be thought through, and not least because sooner or later the retiree will start to depend on them. From the family's point of view, therefore, parents' or grandparents' retirement can come as a mixed blessing. It's not just that they might have turned themselves into SKIers (where SKI = "spending the kids' inheritance"), it's that the extra time they can devote to babysitting now will eventually reverse, and they will need looking after themselves. But as I said at the head of this chapter, that's the point at which the next phase, that of old age, begins.

I also said the phase of retirement was a fuzzy, intermediate one between the beginning of that old age and the end of work, and that retirement might yet involve part-time employment. But for many, the end of work is crystal clear, marked as it is with the traditional retirement party. Like most milestone parties, such as those thrown for weddings or birthdays—parties unimaginable without, say, the cutting of a cake or the blowing out of its candles—the retirement party has a formula of its own. This will include the bestowal of Good Luck cards and the giving of speeches that veer between solemn acknowledgment of your contribution and ribald exposure of your foibles. What's most distinctive about the retirement party, however, is the handing over of the gift. And what could be more classic than the carriage clock or engraved watch? Classic because, as timepieces, they allude to your length of service and, by extension, to your devotion to the job.

Because solidly made, however—a genuine retirement gift can't be flimsy—such timepieces are ironically timeless, suggesting that your retirement will be deservedly long. Perhaps the final irony is this: retirement gives you time, even as the job you're retiring from may have already taken the energy for spending that time away from you.

Happily this grim adage is rarely borne out in reality. A few years into retirement, people will gleefully report how they've been given a new lease on life. If anything, they complain about having too little time, not too much; they even wonder how they ever managed to fit in having a job. It's not just family duties; it's all those long-deferred projects that can finally come to fruition, not to mention new hobbies. A modern and even fleeting phenomenon it might be, but for those lucky enough to enjoy it, retirement represents possibly the best period of life. After all, one might no longer be young, but one is not yet old. And one is free.

18

Living the Third Age

For rescuing Aeneas from Hell, Apollo granted the Sybil, the priestess of the oracle at Cumae, immortality. But there was a catch. For all the Sybil's wisdom, she failed to request the eternal youth necessary to offset the fate she ended up suffering: she simply grew older and older, shrinking further and further until, humiliated, she was kept in a glass jar for all to mock. When a group of boys came to ask her want she wanted, she chillingly replied, "I want to die."

This cautionary tale, an early version of "Be careful what you wish for," enshrines a number of truths about growing old. First, unless you're a Greek god, age and mortality go hand in liver-spotted hand. Were the aging process infinite, were no terminus awaiting you at the end of the line, the very concept of *age* itself would wither. Yes, you would continue to depart temporally from your date of birth, but with no bookend on the other side your age would hardly matter. You might be 53,789 years old, for instance, as would your contemporaries, but with no gauge for telling whether this is spring-chicken-like or old-as-the-hills such data become irrelevant. There'd be people both younger and older than you—some would be millions, even billions of years old—but so what? The only pertinent question would be that raised by the allegory of the Sybil: whether you can age without aging. Assuming, no doubt erroneously, that infinity could contain any such gradations, living forever but gradually subsiding is a very different proposition from living in an unchanged state of "youth." This raises the subquestion of whether "living in an unchanged state" represents a contradiction in terms, on the grounds that life implies change. But the important point is that we will always struggle to conceive of age in isolation from the image of moving toward death.

Not that, second, death might not be desirable. Given that nobody is either immortal or possessed of eternal youth, our later years will be those of steady decline marked by increasing unsteadiness. As Truman Capote said, "Life is a moderately good play with a badly written third act." Without death's grand end-stop, we'd be as desperate and doomed as the Sybil. Looking on the bright side, we could say that death brings blessed relief from the sorrows of decrepitude. It's conceivably a form of mercy, an automatic mechanism that, right at the point we become unviable, puts us out of our misery. Death: the benign usher, if not into infinity, at least out of infirmity.

That said, there's research by the MacArthur Foundation Research Network arguing that, third, the idea of deteriorating faster in later life might be a myth. We might never overcome the existential necessity of death, but with proper diet, exercise, and a positive outlook, we could spend the countdown in pretty good shape. Even the Sybil's bitterness could be mollified, her accursed longevity reinterpreted as something that, instead of deviating irrevocably from eternal youth, does a passable imitation of it. Old age doesn't have to mean a backstage pass into God's waiting room. And this implies an alternative conception of death.

Rather than construing aging as the continuous darkening of a light that will subtly merge into the surrounding blackness, like the signals of a departing airplane blinking out into the night sky, we might envisage a transition far more abrupt but far more zesty: life lived to the max until death swings by with a sudden, catastrophic stroke. It's the difference between a dimmer switch and a strip light, the one fading out, the other snapping off from an almost clinical brightness to an unheralded stop.

Finally, the legend of the Sybil sends out admittedly mixed messages about the connection between age and wisdom. Being a sybil, a veritable seer, she enjoyed the gift of prophecy, a gift that lies in the province of the wise. Despite that, she wasn't wise enough to prophesy what would become of her, nor to see that the offer from Apollo might turn out to be a terrible trap. This results in her condemnation to interminable aging—somewhere today she must still be alive, as minute and friable as a cockroach after a nuclear bomb—a fate that makes her look as foolish as the least wise of all. Once in the desperate position we find her, however, she achieves a second-level wisdom, fabricated out of hindsight and sheer agedness. This is the wisdom of (bitter) experience, and indeed a sense that genuine wisdom can't be had without some prior suffering. In other words, getting wiser as we get older doesn't just come naturally: the wisdom derives from pain and failure. The longer you live, the more pain and failure you'll endure, and thus, in direct proportion, the more wisdom you'll have acquired. You can't be wise without paying.

Nor can you be wise without remembering. Second only to that of death, it's the question of memory that achieves such import in the later years. To state it as a seeming para-

dox: age involves the ruination of memory but the proliferation of memories. Affected increasingly by the discrep-
ancy in effectiveness between long- and short-term memory, the *third age* involves an unlacing of ties to the present
and thus the appearance of detachment. But it would be
fairer to say that the attachment shifts focus onto the past.
After all, the older you get, the more you have to reflect
on and, perhaps proportionally, the less headspace for current matters—though that assumes the brain is a more
fixed entity than it really can be, given our huge capacity
to learn. But what is memory exactly?

It's the other resource that wisdom needs. Authentic wisdom requires converting the experience recalled by memory into insight, and in this respect the concept remains
the same today as it did for Plato and Aristotle. For them,
a distinction applied between learning things by rote,
enabling us to repeat reams of information, and a deeper
learning that penetrated the mind and could make people
genuinely wise. As I said in the chapter on taking exams,
it's possible to cram for the day of the test but retain nothing afterward, which precludes transforming the information into anything sage at all. This is superficial, evanescent
memory. In growing older, by implication, we're almost
destined to become wiser, for what we will have retained
will be those things that have indeed invaded the mind
more deeply, not just been downloaded from the brain for
an immediate challenge, like passing an exam.

The theory sounds fine, except that in later life we recall
not just the weighty events of private and public life—
from divorces to disasters, affairs to assassinations—but
the most trivial incidentals from our youth. "Memory is
like a dog that lies down where it pleases," says the Dutch

author Cees Nooteboom. Such memories might include the license plate number of a friend's car, the brand of perfume worn by an aunt, or the word for *apple* in a foreign language. It's simply not the case that we hang on to only what's important; curios we weren't even trying to recall often stick more stubbornly in the mind than those, like a second cousin's first name or the password to a bank account, we've striven to mentally capture. How to explain such striking inconsistency?

Well if, as Sigmund Freud proposed, the memory's like a wax tablet angled ingenuously toward the world, anything can make an impression on it. It operates with what he called an "evenly suspended attention." Thus the recipe for eggs benedict acquires equal or even more salience than the date of your wedding anniversary. Sure, if challenged, we would readily recognize the anniversary as the more weighty, but our memories don't seem equipped with the same faculty of judgment. What mattered last week, say, was the meeting with the pension adviser and his recommendation to put x percentage of your savings into y fund, but all you can remember is the pattern on his tie. Occasionally this means we'll remember a detail that's vital, but often we won't. Memory appears to be a hopeless judge of what really counts.

The conclusion must be that memory is subjective. Even the pension adviser will recall the meeting differently: you remember his tie, but he can't forget the smell of your aftershave as you opened the door. So what's the explanation? And why is it that, as we get older, there's a persistent set of memories from early youth that keep recurring? A partial explanation lies in the psychoanalytic concept of *cathexis* that Freud proposed somewhat later. For most of the time we glide through the world, wrapped in an invisible cloud of "unbound energy." This energy isn't dissimilar to the erotic because it's a free-floating desire that hasn't yet found an outlet. It's not that we're actively looking for sexual gratification, more that we're in a state of daydreaming, mild detachment, or even boredom, and therefore ready to be seized. After all, we can't be apprehended or interpellated by something new if we're already preoccupied. Out of this miasma state we suddenly latch on to a person's face, the sound of a piano, or the scampering of a dog, and all of that unbound energy flocks to it. Now we have a locus, that upon which we have *cathected*, and are invested.

But if that's how cathexis works, and how we come to have a very singular set of memories, it doesn't yet answer why this tablecloth from your grandmother's house or that boy from summer vacation keep coming back. I said the process is not unerotic; the point of these needle-sharp memories is that, in psychoanalysis at least, they represent a displaced form of something more straightforwardly sexual. That tablecloth bears a subliminal connection to a piece of underwear, the boy to someone physically desired. Our most enduring memory moments, those that recur even late in life, stand for experiences that at their origin had explicitly erotic feelings attached. We might think the third age is characterized by the diminution of libido, but if only in these highly refracted forms, such "energy" persists. And after all, for Freud, *libido* was energy not just for sex but for life more broadly.

You don't need to buy the erotic aspects of cathexis, however, to acknowledge its peculiar power to light on apparently random events and confer upon them instant endurance—not unlike Apollo dispensing immortality to the Sybil. The most famous example must be that in Marcel Proust's *In Search of Lost Time*, where a single bite of a madeleine transports him back to an entire world of his youth. All those disparate memories find themselves corralled at a stroke for their author to enumerate and explore at his uninterrupted leisure. Eventually Marcel, the protagonist, finds himself in a position to reflect back on old age itself. He attends a party and is reunited with many of the characters who have peopled the earlier moments of his vast tapestry of interweaving narratives, and who unknowingly prompt his meditations.

The first of these is that "the phenomenon of old age seemed . . . to take into account certain social habits." What does this mean? Proust talks about the nobleman who ends up looking like the peasants who've worked his fields. In the sense that regardless of upbringing no one can resist it, time is a great leveler, but Proust wants to say rather that the physiognomy of class—the noble brow or the high-bridged nose—itself can be affected, with masters resembling the slaves they once bossed. The older we get, no matter how posh, the more we look like the people with whom we've most associated.

Proust then reflects that among this party of the aged are some notable absences. Owing not to the social or political engagements that formerly took them elsewhere, but to the more absolute appointment with death, the nonattendance of such friends serves as a ticking clock for those attending. He talks about those too infirm to come, and in likening them in their beds to their lying in their "mortuary shrouds," it's clear they'll never be seen again by those who've turned up. Their physical absence conjures up the metaphysical exile soon to define and detain them for good.

Next across his vision parade the ladies of a certain age, accompanied by the vexed question of their physiognomy. Proust constructs three categories, and in the largest he places those women who've refocused their faces around a new feature—like a vineyard, he says, that's been turned over for use as sugar beet. What was the central feature of the face and made up as such—a full mouth, for example—has been downplayed, now that it's caving in, in favor of a still rubicund cheek. Through such pragmatic redress, a certain attractiveness may still be attained. It's worse for the women who populate the other two categories, the ugly and the beautiful. Of the beautiful he says that because their beauty has been as set as a block of marble, all they can do in old age is to crumble away like a statue. As a fate this is actually worse than that of the ugly, who at least can be instantly recognized. "Old age is something human," he says, but "these were monsters, and they no more seemed to have 'changed' than whales." Proust goes on to talk about other guests who appear not to have aged, only to realize it's an illusion. As soon as he gets up close, the impression of smooth skin gives way to what resembles "the surface of a plant or a drop of water or blood when you look at it under a microscope."

Throughout this catalogue of old crones Proust's own combination of fascination and revulsion is what makes his text so compelling. What prevents the scene from collapsing into a simple gallery of grotesque, however, is perhaps the seminal reflection of the novel. Namely, that age permits us not only to note the changes wrought by time, as if inspecting an ancient fresco, but to see things anew. Proust marvels at feeling complete equanimity in the company of an enemy who used to elicit the highest dudgeon. The lesson is that for all the gothic horror evinced by the physiological decay and deformation that accompanies the aging process, the more significant changes occur within.

I talked in the chapter on voting about the half-avowed disquiet that can be caused by changing who you vote for as you get older; typically your views become more conservative. Even if you shift from right to left, a similar self-alienation can occur: Am I really the same person who voted for *X* when I was eighteen? Compared with these huge drifts in the continents of one's sensibility, physical change can appear trivial. There are people who start out generous and end up embittered, and even vice versa. Those once supremely confident become obsequious. Theatrical types turn over time into introverts. Talking about a *self* in such cases seems crude. It's more like we simply reflect the external circumstances we've found ourselves in.

Unfortunately the inner shifts are harder to measure. Where the mirror provides us with a daily report on the thinning of our hair and the thickening of our girths, we lack that mirror's psychological equivalent. This is where friends come in: we should be asking for periodic feedback about how we seem. After all, we ourselves silently make such assessments about those friends. Go for dinner with a mate you've not seen in a while and you'll instantly sense how his or her psychic weather has shifted since the last occasion. This is precious information, too rarely shared.

Except Proust is making a different point. With age comes a new set of (metaphorical) spectacles for looking at the world, even as one's eyesight fails. To feel young, you don't need youth, you need a fresh perspective. For it's the perspective that goes first. It takes only a couple of decades after birth to begin to lose the luminosity of view, the percipient astonishment at what lies around. Typically such renovation of the senses occurs only after a trauma or upon returning home after a lengthy sojourn in a foreign country, but it can also be achieved in increments; reading novels, not least that of Proust, goes some way in changing the world's aspect ratio. To be able to say "I'd never seen it like that before" feels like redeeming part of your life. The experience may not be restricted to the elderly, but it gives them the advantage of feeling relatively younger; that is, they win back more time.

The same applies to the self. While your teeth continue to yellow, your spine to compress, all you need is to be able to see yourself with fresh (again metaphorical) eyes. Certainly you could carry on staring in the mirror every morning with a gentle, irreversible despair, in which case things will worsen only by degrees. Alternatively, you could forgive or even celebrate these alterations of state, conceiving them less as inexorable entropy than as a process of gradual, even wondrous reconfiguration. Easier said than done, perhaps; in Western cultures that champion youth, age has become an inconvenience at the margins. But given that those very cultures are so rapidly aging, it's such margins that will begin to predominate, and unless we're happy to foster a wider mood of self-loathing, our perceptions of age will need to become kinder. Nor are these just changes in perspective. As the very compendiousness of Proust's work makes clear, one has only to look inside one's own mind for infinite worlds to open up. One's skin might be as fretted as a lunar landscape, but the landscape within, which contains one's considerable past as well as one's present, not to mention the whole continent of the imagination, is broader than the world outside. As you physically shrink, the universe within your head can still grow.

So let's give the last word to the great English literary critic and poet William Empson and offset a fraction of this prejudice. If it's only the young who seem entitled to a place in the sun, let them have it. That moon holds more beauty, and it hangs in its pale coolness as a fitting lozenge of old age. Thus Empson's poem "To an Old Lady" begins, "Ripeness is all; her in her cooling planet/Revere; do not presume to think her wasted." The old lady is both the moon and a moon-like old lady. Where we might conceive aging as Sybil-like desiccation, here Empson gestures to a perpetual fullness. Hence quoting Shakespeare's line "Ripeness is all." Although her planet might be cooling, it should not therefore be mocked, but revered. The phrase "cooling planet" has a brittle, silvery wonder to it, far less brassy than that of the hot sun. Age might involve being periodically eclipsed by the world, but in its capacity to endure, even if not forever, it retains a dignity that can't be gainsaid, so "do not presume to think her wasted." Delicate it might appear, but the moon keeps rising.

19

Going Out in Style

In distinguishing biography from autobiography, the deciding factor must surely be that the former treats of a different person, whereas the latter concerns the self. This doesn't mean that biographers aren't routinely accused of painting too much of themselves into their subject, thus autobiographizing the biography and compromising its otherwise objective point of view. But the two genres as such remain distinct. Just as obviously, an autobiography can be written by only one specific person, its own subject, in contrast to biography, which extends a writing license to all and sundry. Again, you could quibble: less literate autobiographers sometimes turn to ghost writers to lend a hand, thus pluralizing the authorial voice. But such hired help will generally do whatever it can to efface itself and thus strengthen the singularity of the autobiographer's own self-reflection.

Often overlooked, however, is the deeper fissure dividing these two literary forms, defining them just as decisively. Whereas a biography can report on the death of its subject, an autobiography certainly cannot. Sure, many biographies get written with the biographee still breathing, but that's just a matter of timing; were the living subject to die during the biography's composition, there'd be no problem, in principle, with adding the extra chapter post-mortem. But of autobiography the same cannot be averred: the death of the writer is the end of the text. Right up until the last gasp of life the author might be scribbling, but when that life gives over, so too the autobiographical project must reach its conclusion. Finis.

Does this imply that no autobiography is ever done? Perhaps. More can always be added anyway, regardless of how close to death the autobiography was penned. But if death can't be included in the story of one's life, what kind of an autobiography does it make? Not only is it less objective than the biography, but it's less complete. Yet this assumes death to be a part of life, an assumption for which we have biographies themselves partly to blame. A biographer of a deceased person feels duty-bound to describe the death, and we readers have come to expect such concluding comments as a necessary rounding-off. Without them the biography feels like a sentence without a full stop

Which makes us uncomfortable, does it not? A life, like the story I was describing in chapter 1, asks for an ending. But when it comes to dying, the paradox is that we do not undergo it. Autobiographer or not, the experience of dying is no experience at all, for the redoubtable reason that death signals the ending of experience. Up until you die all is experience, but death, by definition, never encroaches into the lifeworld. Your last breath and last rites might count as fields of experience, but death begins only when such finalities, like you, desist. This assumes, of course, that death should be set apart from what it looks like in the movies: the last flickerings of light, the final judderings of breath. In talking about a "moment" of death, and especially of a "tunnel," therefore, we're too vague: there's life followed by not-life, without transition between them and without any possibility of the subject in question witnessing the contrast.

If death can be observed by everybody except its victim, this isn't the only separator between a dying person and those in attendance. Just as an autobiography can't finally or fully be outsourced to those aptly named ghost writers, so one's death remains as inalienable as one's shadow. Tempting as it may be, you can't get anyone to die your death for you. Equally, you can't die for someone else. Though a father, say, might sacrifice himself to save his son, it's still the father's death that the father dies. So let's not be vague about the notion of sacrifice either! For the sake of someone else, you might agree to stop living, but you might well hesitate before letting yourself die his or her death, especially if it's grisly.

When it comes to death, nobody can take your place, which perhaps defines what a milestone is after all: a staging post that can't be avoided, despite the fact that some of the milestones I've detailed in this book will be discretionary. It's a solemn truth captured in the old gospel blues "Lonesome Valley," from the Deep South of America, which tells people they need to go to the lonesome valley "by yo'self. Nobody else can go for you." Right up to the final nanoseconds of existence you might be safely accompanied, but when the lights go out and it's time to make the journey, you're on your own. Death means nothing if not leaving others behind.

Needless to say, the valley in the song alludes to and adapts the famous Twenty-third Psalm: "Yea, though I walk through the valley of the shadow of death, I will fear no evil: For thou art with me." Given the sheer lonesomeness of that passage, it's hardly surprising that we might look for comfort in a Lord acting as our shepherd, nor that people often turn closer to religion the further death hoves into view. Strictly speaking, the psalm seems to be saying that the valley of the shadow of death is the shadow cast by death over our life: our mortality demands that, even at the high noon of our being, we walk in darkness. But this correction scarcely changes the sentiment. Both the prospect and the inevitability of death can surely be denied or ignored, or they can be fearlessly faced, but most of us never quite do either, and, peering down into that valley, we might well reach for a hand to hold, especially if it belongs to God.

In response to which, there's plenty of skepticism to be gathered. First, the God-as-shepherd image renders God the mere personification of our need for solace—a grandiose way of saying that we're weak. There's no shepherd even though we bleat like sheep. Second, just as there's no God to cosset you, nor is there any "valley." This too amounts to nothing more than an image, a poetic brocade for covering up the fact that life does indeed just stop, like a film without epilogue or sequel. Third, turning to religion the moment death comes knocking feels like a cop-out, or a last-minute cop-in. Can a deathbed conversion really make up for a life of venality? If it can, why don't we just party all day and, just before the bell of midnight tolls, make a swift atonement?

Actually, between the dovish position of trusting in the celestial shepherd and the hawkish one telling you to get over yourself, you don't have to choose—or rather, you can choose to believe and still come off looking pretty savvy.

Just follow the advice of Blaise Pascal: devout seventeenth-century Christian philosopher he may have been, but he devised a formula for religious belief that was ingeniously hard-headed. Known as "Pascal's wager," it argued that the consequences of partying and not ultimately turning to God would be infinitely less preferable than upholding a faith. How so? If God does exist—and nobody knows for sure—then spending your life believing in Him can be cashed in for a berth in heaven. Your earthly goodliness will find its just desert in everlasting bliss. But if God exists and you fritter that life away with the wantonness of an infidel, He's going to make sure you go to Hell. As far as worst-case scenarios go, that pretty much takes the honors. On balance, therefore, living a religious life is the best—or the least bad—bet. Instead of fire and brimstone, the worst outcome, if God proves to be a fiction, is nothingness and the personal satisfaction of having lived a decent existence.

Melding simplicity with guile, this suave Pascalian logic implies that deathbed contrition comes a little late. The more orthodox Christian view allows last-minute pleadings, but in Pascal the last few moments of life offer only so much virtue to be begged, and that means turning up at the pearly gates with the meagerest of spiritual worth. Don't be surprised if St. Peter waves you contemptuously away. Indeed the logic, so hard to argue with, effectively demands that you start your spiritual exercises from the moment you become apprised of the logic. In this sense, the analogy with money, otherwise so inapposite for the threshold between heaven and earth, rings even truer. The earlier you start saving, the better, as the return on investment is potentially infinite. Death gets cast as the inscrutable but scrupulously fair cashier who ensures that everyone gets back just what goodness they've banked.

What's wrong with the analogy, however, is its suggestion of varying grades of heavenly joy, like ascending levels of club membership. With such a pecking order, heaven wouldn't be so heavenly. It evokes the dubious selectivity propounded by less mainstream parts of the church, such as Jehovah's Witnesses, Promise Keepers, and Scientologists, all of whom, in ways that mimic or inspire far-right politics, preach a vision of God's kingdom that has room for only so many. But it nevertheless reinforces the notion of death as a day of judgment, and for all Pascal's subtlety, there's an absoluteness in this that he would probably endorse. Yes, we can evaluate our lives en passant and there will be many milestones—this book describes the majority of them—that prompt such taking stock. But just as the biography becomes more complete the more it incorporates of the life it details, so the assessment of an individual achieves proper robustness only once that life, like a case file, has closed. Not to mention the fact that deceased's legacy, be it manifested as children or works, will continue to reflect on them after their death.

But what are the criteria for such an assessment? When it comes to our personal self-reckoning we'll no doubt employ similar techniques of appraisal; regardless of how diverse the life that's been lived, its end offers up a highly generic set of descriptors. Have you been good or bad? Loving or mean? A success or a failure? Formulaic though they sound, such measures do help us to highlight the important stuff. The difference is that where a biography or its little brother, the obituary, focus on what's externally significant, one's own personal review will nearly always light on the emotions. It's less one's achievements—gaining high rank, winning a prize—that will come to the fore than the loves and the losses.

We know this not least through grief, the other means by which we are practiced in death before we encounter the real thing. Of course, as Seneca pointed out, you can never actually rehearse your own death before dying, because to do so would be to die. But the death of others at least offers a few clues. When we grieve, it's not for the deceased's ability on the French horn, her magna cum laude from Harvard, or his having won the Tokyo marathon. Grief couldn't be less related to assessment; the bereft and the biographer represent utterly different species. Death causes sorrow, the suffering that each of us will helplessly inflict on our loved ones when we die, and that, ironically, we will be spared.

Sorrow, however, is too bland a word for the nuances of the grieving process, a process broken down into discreet phases by the Swiss psychiatrist Elisabeth Kübler-Ross in her seminal 1969 book, *On Death and Dying*. Of these phases there are five:

1. Denial
2. Anger
3. Bargaining
4. Depression
5. Acceptance

Apart from *bargaining*, they're all self-evident. When a loved one dies, you pretend it hasn't happened, then you rail against it, you slump into deep sadness, and ultimately you come to terms. Bargaining is the odd one out because it pertains more to people who are dying than to those who will grieve for them. That said, even after someone has passed away, you can bargain with God to bring him or her back by offering up your own life instead.

It was through working with the terminally ill at clinics in the United States that Kübler-Ross originally developed her model as the "five psychological stages of dying"; that is, it was about approaching one's own death rather than someone else's. Among other things she noticed that as death gets nearer, people will conceive wagers, not a million miles from Pascal's, to be allowed to live a little longer. Wagers such as "I'll believe in you, God, if you just let me live" or "I'll take more pain, but don't let me die yet." And of course, one might strike similar bargains for someone else: "Please don't let her die: I'll do anything!" Clearly the model lends itself to various uses and, even though Kübler-Ross noted that one phase would sometimes overlap with another or perhaps be skipped, the notion of the emotions following a change curve has taken root in popular consciousness.

Take *Three Colours Blue*, the 1993 film by the Polish director Krzysztof Kieślowski, starring Juliette Binoche. Riding with them in the same car, Binoche's character survives her husband and daughter, who are both killed in a crash. When she comes around in the hospital and realizes her loss, she tries to take her own life. This, if you like, is a form of *denial*, but one so extreme it effectively becomes its opposite: it's precisely because she accepts so clearly the truth of the two deaths, because she sees the horror and desperation of it so starkly, that she lunges at this final solution for herself. Without her family, her life has lost all meaning, so in killing herself she's not really killing anything at all; she died in the crash too. In terms of grief's phases, this might mark a phase zero, preceding even denial. Alternatively, it's a denial in that, if she dies too, it's as if her husband and child have not.

Before long she passes into a new phase, but it's worth a paragraph on this doleful question of suicide. You are now reading the last chapter of this book, with the subject of death coming after events like marriage and moving house. So I'm talking about a natural death taking place at the end of a long life, but of course death can occur much earlier, either by chance or by design. We tend to believe that our death lies beyond our control, that it will occur at some unspecified point in the future, but the truth is it's entirely in our hands. Or rather, it's entirely in our hands to bring it forward. We can never be completely assured of putting it off because, like the husband and daughter in the film, we continue our lives at the mercy of fatal accidents that come out of the blue and rob of us of the future we'd hazily been anticipating. Suicide cuts across time, cuts it out. It takes charge of time, making certain the uncertainty of death. Recognizing that she, like all of us, has this power at her disposal, Binoche's character decides to snatch it. But in offering such a shortcut out of life, it might also be that her attempted suicide constitutes an effort less at leaving than at joining—that is, at reuniting with her family on the other side.

It fails, and she embarks on the next of an extended series of phases that do and don't map onto those of Kübler-Ross. One involves divesting herself of all her worldly possessions; another, a passionate fling that, rather than betraying her husband's memory, strangely honors it, precisely because it's a mode of grief, a means of dealing with the loss. The point being that when we die, we tap out a series of waves through the emotional system to which we hitherto belonged. We continue to affect those who survive us, distorting their behavior and, in a perfectly nonsupernatural sense, haunting them. We may pass away, but for a generation or two we live on in the hearts and the minds of the living.

Put another way, death may be abrupt—it might be that instantaneous switchover from life to nonlife—but when that instant falls, our lives get refracted spectrally into the lives of those who've yet to run up against their own last instant. In this view, it would be more accurate to speak not of the pair *life and death*, but of a trinity, *life, haunting, and death*, as the great stages of the soul. Only when our descendants have forgotten us for good do we finally die. Death befalls us about a century after death, giving us plenty of time—about a lifetime, as it happens—to get used to it.

Perhaps this draws some of the sting from death. We abandon our life but, at the point of death, transmit that life, or pictures of it, into the memories of those who care. Thus death becomes the subset rather than the antagonist of life. It's a thought that would have found the support of Arthur Schopenhauer, the great if somewhat neglected German philosopher of the nineteenth century. He wrote of the whole world—animal, mineral, and vegetable—as animated by a fundamental striving, or a *will* (a will that inspired the thoughts of Nietzsche that I covered in relation to midlife crisis). Be it a human being or a tree, each wants to affirm and prolong its being-there. There's an energy that gives life to the tree and the human, and this energy persists even after they have passed away. It's what animates the next generation of trees and people, such that the expiration of one individual pales in comparison with this larger, perpetual surge.

Put that back into the context of human life and death, and you can see that the dying of one person will sustain negligible impact on the will of life—or Life—to keep living. Not only that, but dying allows a replenishment or regeneration of that will. If, like the Sybil in the previous chapter, we were to live into perpetuity, it would be accompanied by an unavoidable degradation. Death allows life to reboot. Sure, that's a bummer for the individual, who does actually have to die, but from the point of view of life, it's fairly miraculous. Death serves the vitality of life, bows down to the general will, which represents the profoundest urge that exists in the world. It even helps explain why there is something rather than nothing: the universe didn't have to come about, so there must have been an x that was more than neutral, something affirmative and self-interested, to get it going. For which the term *will* might not be so inaccurate.

All this relieves death from a portion of the tragedy we often attribute to it and gives the notion of "going out in style" some genuine credibility. Because our exit allows others to enter, we might feel that our lives weren't lived in vain, that the animating spirit has, like a torch, been passed on. There's a generosity in this, and no reason it can't be translated into how one lives out one's final days. You can die crabbed, wizened, and embittered, but you can also bow out with a flourish that recognizes you've had the gift of life and that now you're making a gift of it to others in turn. This frees you up to die well, a notion that we in the West are less attuned to than those in the East. In fixating on the art of living, we tend to leave death until the last moment, as though it takes care of itself. Perhaps it's a belief that fails to respect a duty we may have, as we lie dying, to finish adroitly.

You have only to look at the *Tibetan Book of the Dead* to realize that other cultures treat dying as an equivalent test, and that the art of living lies partly in preparing for its closure. It can include specific techniques, such as lucent dreaming, those waking dreams we might produce at dawn that supposedly anticipate the hallucinatory states we shall experience in any transition (if there is one, despite my earlier comments) between life and death. If we can practice this habit, we'll be more alert in this moment of postexistential crisis to dangers that may waylay us.

For the dying process makes us vulnerable. The passage from here to the afterlife might be strewn with terrors; you have only to visit those royal tombs that furnish their inhabitants with armor and treasures for the journey to realize it. Even if we've lived a good life, it's possible we'll get blown off course and never reach the hallowed destination. I began by speaking of life as a journey, but it's not inconceivable—after all, nobody alive has any proof—that death will also demand we forge a passage. It mightn't be as extreme or dramatic a choice as that between heaven and hell, but the passage into our resting place might yet be forked. Indeed the routes and the destinations could be manifold. In which case, reflecting on death might be less a gratuitous and more an essential part of life. So who would contradict the saying of Montaigne, that to philosophize is to learn how to die? As he explains:

That is because study and contemplation draw our souls somewhat outside ourselves, keeping them occupied away from the body, a state which both resembles death and which forms a kind of apprenticeship for it; or perhaps it is because all the wisdom and argument in the world eventually come down to one conclusion; which is to teach us not to be afraid of dying.

AFTERLIFE

> There are three deaths. The first is when the body
> ceases to function. The second is when the body is
> consigned to the grave. The third is that moment,
> sometime in the future, when your name is spoken
> for the last time.

I quote from David Eagleman's *Sum: Forty Tales from the Afterlives*, which does what it says on the jacket, offering forty imaginary accounts of what life will be like after the Grim Reaper has made his visit. The fact that there are forty of these accounts doesn't matter; it could have been fifty or eighty or eight thousand. When it comes to the afterlife, there's no limit on our imaginings about it, precisely because it exists on the other side of life, beyond empirical reach. No one as yet has been there and returned with a report that has then been corroborated, so imagination is the *only* grasp of it we have. If nowhere else, the afterlife exists in that precinct of our brain dedicated to speculation and belief. The afterlife lives inside us. In a sense, it's a work of fiction, not unlike Eagleman's book. This isn't to claim that there's no such thing as a real afterlife, but that all we can talk about when we talk about the afterlife is something we've constructed to represent it.

This make-believe afterlife is often imagined in one of

two ways: it's either a final destination for the deceased human being, such as a heaven or a hell, or it's a transitional phase between incarnations. In both cases, it's not the human being who inhabits the afterlife—he or she is dead, after all—but a proxy, such as a soul, a spirit, or a ghost. That said, some Christian theologians talk of the "resurrection of the body," as though we wake up again as ourselves, as after a long nap. But even if the body makes it through to the other side, it will have been transfigured by its now occupying the realm of the divine: the body becomes spirit.

To atheists, this is all mumbo-jumbo. The afterlife isn't just fictitious, it's laughable. At best it's a fantasy to console us in the face of the nothingness that follows upon death; at worst, it's an alibi for religions to manipulate their followers. No, we are bound to the earth, not just in the way I described in the chapter on walking—glued winglessly to the surface of the planet—but our bodies remain in or on that planet long after we've deceased. The corpse might emit its gases, but nothing like a spirit ever floats up and away from the mortal remains.

Nevertheless the belief in an afterlife—and it is only ever a belief—can bring benefits. I talked in the previous chapter about Pascal's wager, which argues that you're better off believing in God, because the consequences of not doing so (Hell) don't bear thinking about. There's also the doctrine of karma, the idea that your next life can be influenced by your actions in the present; this can be understood in a Pascalian fashion, as follows. Let's agree that nobody actually knows if there's an afterlife or not. If there really is, and you live an immoral life, then in the next one you're going to be faced with misery. Alternatively, if you live a moral life, and there's nothing after it, at least you'll have enjoyed the appreciation of those around you. In this argument, it's worth *believing* in an afterlife; after all, you can't prove it doesn't exist. Besides, what does a belief cost you? We're only dealing with intangibles.

Ironically, therefore, the main function of the afterlife as it is imagined might have less to do with what comes *after* life and more to do with our lives right here, right now, and how we live them. Which effectively makes *the afterlife* another name for conscience, that internal barometer we're fitted with at birth that guides us in making moral choices. As I said in the introduction, several of the milestones we pass—such as learning to walk—are both physical and more or less inevitable, and so call for little moral reflection. But many—such as getting married or choosing a career—are not foregone conclusions, and it's these relatively discretionary rites of passage that can benefit from such an instrument as conscience. Whether you believe in an afterlife or not, your conscience plays the paradoxical role in the present of looking at you in hindsight, as if reflecting back on your life after its surcease. It asks, "Will this have been a good decision?"

So even though we have no evidence for the afterlife, it works like conscience works—as a way of posing questions about how we conduct ourselves in the here and now. In effect, this means that the afterlife also works like philosophy works, getting you to reflect in real time on the larger implications of your actions. At least, this is the way philosophy has conceived its task since Socrates and his most famous pupil, Plato, began to enquire into what Hannah Arendt, as we know, later called "the human condition." Yes, to philosophize is to learn how to die, as Montaigne said, but it's also to learn how to live.

FURTHER READING

Althusser, Louis. *Politics and History: Montesquieu, Rousseau, Marx.* Verso, 2007.

Barthes, Roland. *A Lover's Discourse.* Vintage, 2002.

Coetzee, J. M. *Slow Man.* Vintage, 2006.

Heidegger, Martin. *Basic Writings.* Routledge, 2003.

Hume, David. *An Enquiry concerning Human Understanding.* Oxford World's Classics, 2008.

Joyce, James. *Finnegans Wake.* Penguin Classics, 2000.

Kerouac, Jack. *On the Road.* Penguin Modern Classics, 2007.

Kierkegaard, Søren. *The Essential Kierkegaard.* Princeton, 2000.

Kübler-Ross, Elisabeth. *On Death and Dying.* Routledge, 2008.

Le Corbusier. *Towards a New Architecture.* BN Publishing, 2008.

Milton, John. *The Major Works.* Oxford World's Classics, 2008.

Pascal, Blaise. *Pensées and Other Writings.* Oxford World's Classics, 2008.

Phillips, Adam. *On Kissing, Tickling and Being Bored.* Faber, 1993.

Plato. *The Collected Dialogues.* Princeton, 1961.

Ricoeur, Paul. *Oneself as Another.* Chicago, 1994.

Sartre, Jean-Paul. *Being and Nothingness: An Essay on Phenomenological Ontology.* Routledge, 2003.

Woolf, Virginia. *A Room of One's Own.* Penguin Classics, 2002.

INDEX

INDEX

INDEX

INDEX

ABOUT THE AUTHOR

Robert Rowland Smith spent the first part of his career as a Prize Fellow of All Souls College, Oxford, and the second as a partner in a leading firm of management consultants. He has lectured around the world on philosophy, literature, and psychoanalysis; written for many newspapers and magazines; and broadcast for BBC Radio. He has a column in the *Sunday Times Magazine* on moral dilemmas. Having lived in Oxford, France, and Los Angeles, he has returned to his native London. His last book was the highly acclaimed *Breakfast with Socrates*.